Living Water

Living Water

✦

The Spirit-Filled Life

Norman Bell

iUniverse, Inc.
New York   Bloomington

Living Water
The Spirit-Filled Life

The views expressed in this work are solely those of the author and do not necessarily
reflect the views of the publisher, and the publisher hereby disclaims any responsibility
for them.

iUniverse books may be ordered through booksellers or by contacting:

iUniverse
1663 Liberty Drive
Bloomington, IN 47403
www.iuniverse.com
1-800-Authors (1-800-288-4677)

Because of the dynamic nature of the Internet, any Web addresses or links contained
in this book may have changed since publication and may no longer be valid.

ISBN: 978-1-4502-0035-6 (sc)
ISBN: 978-1-4502-0037-0 (dj)
ISBN: 978-1-4502-0036-3 (ebk)

Printed in the United States of America

iUniverse rev. date: 12/28/2009

Table of Contents

Preface

After the encouragement from several friends, I have undertaken to share, with those who might read this book, the truth as I have learned it about our wonderful Comforter and Counselor, the Sweet Spirit of Christ.

I have been preaching these truths in revivals, seminars, Bible conferences, and as a pastor for over 40 years. The Spirit of God has made them a blessing to many people. It is my hope that they will be an equal blessing to you.

I had never considered writing these truths in a book until a recent Bible Conference at a large church in Tennessee. Having been strongly encouraged to write them, I was unable to get away from the idea for the first time. So after weeks of praying and searching for the will of our heavenly Father, I have put forth this effort.

Throughout the book I have used the King James Version of the Bible. The reason for this is simple. It is the version in which I learned the Word of God. It is familiar to me. I read many other versions and translations, and they are a great help.

I have sought to honor God the Father, Son, and Holy Spirit by using caps in referring to either of them, in noun or pronoun. The exception to this rule is when I am quoting scripture. Then I try to put it just like it is in the Bible. All proper names are to be capitalized, but not necessarily pronouns. Please try to understand, that even though this practice may not be the norm for writing, it is done in this book to indicate my reverence for the Persons of the Godhead. I have also capitalized the phrase, the "Word of God" for a similar reason.

I have read many, many books on the ministry of the Holy Spirit in the 50 years of my ministry. I am sure that many or most of my concepts and convictions about the ministry of the Holy Spirit were arrived at as a result of reading my brothers' works. I am deeply grateful to them for the great contribution they have made to my life and ministry. But this work is mine, therefore I take full responsibility for all the mistakes, goofs, and all other errors in the book.

May Almighty God, Creator of this universe in which we live, edify you through the ministry of the Holy Spirit as you, hopefully, study these glorious truths. If you are a teacher, or preacher, please feel free to use them in your lessons or sermons.

Norman S. Bell

Introduction

I grew up in eastern North Carolina. My parents named me Norman My sixteen year old sister nicknamed me Jack the day I was born and it stuck. I still go by that name to all of my friends and family. I came to Christ when I was 30 plus years old. I graduated from Fruitland Baptist Bible Institute with honors. I graduated from North Greenville College cum laude with an A.A in Liberal Arts. I graduated from Luther Rice Bible College and Seminary with a B.M. I pastured churches in North Carolina, South Carolina and New York. I served as a Director of Missions of the North American Mission Board in Adirondack Baptist Association until I retired. While serving there, I was privileged to serve on several state and national committees.

During this time I was also privileged by my fellow pastors to preach many revivals and conferences in their churches on the subject of this book. Since retiring, I have continued to have invitations to preach in churches large and small with tremendous results. I also led a conference on the Spirit-filled life at the Southern Baptist National Assembly at Ridgecrest in the mountains of North Carolina. What a joy it all has been.

I served in the armed forces during WWII in the paratroopers, but I was only in for 25 months.

My hobbies have been reading, travel and woodworking. Much of the travel was by RV in 49 of the fifty states, but I had to fly to Hawaii. I have enjoyed traveling in Europe, Greece and Israel.

I was married to Lena Leonard and we had three children. One son is deceased and the other serves as Minister of Evangelism at Vaughn Forest Baptist Church in Montgomery, Alabama. The daughter is married to Nathan Blackwell, pastor of Cornerstone Church in St. Cloud, Florida. They minister to several thousand people.

After my first wife's death, I married Carrie Burns of Tucson, Arizona. We have lived here for the past 8 years in which time I did this writing.

Norman S. Bell

Chapter 1

What Is The Spirit-Filled Life

I had been a believer for only five months. I had been converted from an anti-Christian, anti-church person to an ardent follower of Jesus. I was leading the music in the Newport Baptist Church in Newport, N.C. after a powerful Spirit-filled sermon. During the invitation to commitment to Christ as Lord I had an overwhelming hunger and thirst for God to have all of me. Suddenly I began to weep for no apparent reason. I couldn't control the weeping. As I wept I became weaker and weaker. To keep from falling I got down on my knees. It seemed as if wave after wave of liquid love was sweeping over me. I became so weak that I lay prostrate on the floor. The waves continued to roll over me. I was so weak that I couldn't lift an arm. The feelings I was experiencing were pure ecstasy and joy.

When my strength returned, everyone else had left the church. I didn't know what had happened to me. I only knew that it was good and of God. Immediately following this experience I began to experience the fruit of the Spirit--- love, joy, peace, longsuffering, gentleness, goodness, faith, meekness, temperance-- in my life. The message of the Bible came a live to me. Jesus became more real to me. The Christian life became so exciting.

Sometime later I was reading Dr. R.A. Torrey's book, THE HOLY SPIRIT, WHO HE IS AND WHAT HE DOES. (Dr. Torrey was president of Moody Bible Institute, pastor of the Moody church in Chicago, and a world evangelist.) In the book he described the filling or baptism of the Holy Spirit. It described precisely what happened to me. I now knew what my experience was. The results of my experience are still with me fifty-six years later. I have made a thorough study of the subject from the Bible and from other authors, and have spent much of my ministry seeking to help others understand this beautiful truth. That is what this book is about.

To be filled with the Spirit is an experience and an event like being saved is. What happened to me was this. I had been saved and received the Spirit at the time of my salvation. I had received all of the Spirit. He is a Person and is not divided into pieces so that I get a little now and a little more later. Because I wanted God to have all of me, I had opened my life for Him to take control of every area of it. He invaded every room in my personal life. I was full of Him. I had experienced the "fullness of the Godhead bodily."

Have you ever read about the power of the Holy Spirit in the book of Acts and wondered why you did not experience some of the same things they did? These things were happening to them because they had been filled with the Holy Spirit. They understood scriptures they had never understood before. They were no longer intimidated by the powers that were. They felt total freedom to act and did.

Do you read your Bible and wish you could understand it better? Do you ever pray and feel that your prayer got no higher than the ceiling? Do you often feel defeated in your walk with Christ? Do you seem unable to break the strongholds in your life? The secret to overcoming all of this is to be filled with and walk in the Holy Spirit.

I have heard much about the fact that believers needed to be filled with the Spirit of God for living and ministry. Very few ever told HOW to be filled with the Holy Spirit.

This book is about HOW to be filled with the Holy Spirit and HOW to walk in the Spirit so that we will not fulfill the lust of the flesh. Gal. 5:16. But first let us look at what the Spirit-filled life is all about.

In the years immediately following the day of Pentecost the Spirit-filled life was normal for the believer. To not be filled was considered abnormal. In today's church to be filled with the Holy Spirit is so rare that it is often considered abnormal. The Spirit-filled life is the birth right of every true believer in Jesus Christ. God has purposed, promised and provided for every true believer to be filled with and walk in the Spirit. In my lifetime of Bible study, I have found that the Spirit-filled life will result at least in the following characteristics:

THE ABUNDANT LIFE

In John 10:10b, Jesus told His followers that "I am come that you might have life, and have it more abundantly." It seems to me that Jesus is promising two things rather than repeating one thing in this verse. The two things He promises are *life* and the *abundant life.*

To be born again is what Jesus was promising as "life." To be born again means to have a spiritual birth in addition to our physical birth. As the physical birth is necessary to live the physical life, so is the spiritual birth necessary to live the Christian or spiritual life. Jesus said that when a person experiences this spiritual birth he is born again. He explained how this happens in John's gospel.

¹⁴ "And as Moses lifted up the serpent in the wilderness, even so must the Son of man be lifted up: ¹⁵ That whosoever believeth in him should not perish, but have eternal life. ¹⁶ For God so loved the world, that he gave his only begotten Son, that whosoever believeth in him should not perish, but have everlasting life. ¹⁷ For God sent not his Son into the world to condemn the world; but that the world through him might be saved." John 3:14-17

A person is born again as a result of believing in his heart that Jesus is who He says He is. He then invites Jesus into his heart to forgive and save him.

Every born again believer has life. Jesus is that life. (Col. 3:4.) Jesus dwells in every believer in the person of the Holy Spirit or the Spirit of Christ which is one and the same.

"If any man have not the Spirit of Christ, he is none of His." Rom. 8:9.

So then every believer has life. But does every believer "have it more abundantly"? The abundant life results from the Spirit-filled life. It is the quality of life. In many years of observation in my Christian walk, I have seen so many Christians defeated, depressed, disappointed, discouraged, and divided. They certainly do not manifest that they have life "more abundantly" or filled with the Spirit. More often than not, so many seem to be wearied in their walk with Christ. There is very little difference in their attitude toward life than the people who are not believers.

The liver of the abundant life is excited about God being his Lord and Savior. He senses and knows that God is very active in his daily life. He believes that God is working "all things together for good" in his life. This is because he loves Him and is called according to His purpose. He is joyous and full of love for God and fellow man. He is generally victorious in his life and walk. He stands out among the brethren. He is "salt" and "light" to the unredeemed. God wants all His people to experience the abundant life. Christ died so that you could not only have life, but have it MORE ABUNDANTLY which implies not only quantity but quality. Another characteristic of the Spirit-filled life is the abiding life.

THE ABIDING LIFE

Jesus said in John 15:4-5, "Abide in me, and I in you. As a branch cannot bear fruit of itself, except it abide in the vine, no more can you except you abide in me. I am the vine, you are the branches: He that abideth in me and I in him, the same bringeth forth much fruit, for without me you can do nothing."

I understand Jesus to be saying that He is our source of power to bear fruit, more fruit, and much fruit. He is the true vine and we are the branches. The branches on a vine draw ALL their sap from the vine. That enables them to bear fruit. Likewise we must draw all our strength from Christ to enable us to bear fruit. We do this by abiding in Him.

To abide generally means to dwell. To abide in Christ is to be saved and include Him in everything about our life. It is to ask His will in all that we do. The abider in Christ has no area of life that isn't under Christ's control. He has no known un-confessed sin. Christ always abides in the believer. When the believer abides in Him he is conscious of Jesus' presence with him.

How do I go about making sure that I am abiding in Christ? The abiding life has no un-confessed sin and disobedience in it. The abiding believer confesses any and all sin immediately upon committing it. We know immediately that we have sinned because the Holy Spirit is grieved. We feel His grief. Immediate confession of our sin allows our fellowship with our Lord to proceed uninterrupted. Upon confession, we are forgiven and cleansed. To not repent of and confess our sin immediately stops the flow of our fellowship with God and His Spirit in us is grieved. He then no longer has control of our entire life.

The abiding life has no corner or area of life into which Jesus is not brought. He is Lord of ALL of life. There is no life in which He cannot share. To abide in Christ is to make Him Lord of the way we dress, use our material wealth and belongings. It is to make Him Lord of our pleasure activities, our attitudes, how we treat our fellowman, how we serve our employers, how we treat our families, and everything else.

The abiding life is a life that looks to Jesus for all wisdom needed for life, for answers to life's problems, and that follows His plan for our life. It seeks to be obedient to the Word of God in every situation whether it seems the wise thing to us or not.

"Trust in the Lord with all thine heart, and lean not unto thine own understanding, but in all thy ways acknowledge Him, and He shall direct thy paths." (Prov. 3:5-6)

The abiding life is the Christ centered and Christ controlled life. We attain this by listening to the Spirit of Christ who is in us and the Word of Christ which He has given us. The Spirit of Christ is always RESIDENT in a believer's life. We have to MAKE HIM PRESIDENT of our life. We must make a decision by our will to make Him president. That means that whatsoever we do, we do it just like we were doing it in His presence and for Him. (Col. 3:23.) Christ, not material things, is the focus and center of one's thought and activities.

Still another characteristic of the Spirit-filled life is the overflowing life.

THE OVERFLOWING LIFE

Jesus said, "If any man thirst, let him come unto me and drink. He that believeth on me as the scriptures have said, out of his belly (inner life) shall flow rivers of living water. This spake He of the Spirit..." (John 7:37-38.)

The absolute requirement for the filling of the Holy Spirit is a hunger and thirst for God. Like the Psalmist David, our soul must thirst and long for the living God. (Psalms 42:1-3 and 63:1-2) Jesus told us that if we have that kind of thirst, we are to come unto Him and drink. Drinking is simply the process by which we get what we want from the outside of us into the inside of us. In this case we drink by believing every word of Jesus and the scriptures. When we so drink, we begin flowing over on others.

Notice that we do not "flow" a trickle, but rivers. Not just small streams but rivers (plural) of living water as suggested by the cover design of the book. The words of Jesus here are in the present tense, which means to drink and keep on drinking, continuously. This rules out an occasional drink. And as long as we drink we flow. Have you ever been around a "flowing" believer? To a carnal believer, a flowing believer can be a threat and an unpleasant experience. This is true because the carnal believer has no idea what the overflowing is about and it is far beyond his concepts of the Christian life. Generally the overflowing believer is a joy and a blessing to others. Are you experiencing the overflowing life? You can be.

Years ago I had a college student from Memphis, Tenn., come to work with me in New York State for the summer, sight unseen. When I picked him up in Syracuse I was shocked at his appearance. He had long hair and a beard. He was wearing bib overalls. One suspender was unfastened and hung down. He wore no shirt. He was barefooted as well, and had one pants' leg rolled up to the knee. He was laughing and praising God so loudly that I thought that I had something I didn't want on my hands. I got another surprise. He really did love Jesus. He really was serious in his thirst for more of God. He would come with his Bible and sit on the floor in front of me and say. "Pastor Bell, teach me God's Word." It didn't seem to matter what portion of the Bible, or what doctrine I taught. He searched the scriptures with me. After an hour or so of this, he would go to his room and review what I had taught him until he had it straight. Then he would immediately go out on the street and find someone to tell the truths he had learned

Mark Gold had come to stay with me for only ten weeks. He wound up staying for three years. His life was continuously overflowing on me, and everyone he was around. He had discovered and practiced the truth of the overflowing life. Everyone loved Mark. Mark enrolled in the State University of New York to finish his degree.

I lived 30 miles from campus. Mark had a car to drive to campus, but he chose to hitch- hike so he could witness to the persons giving him a ride. He did this when the temperature was 20 and 30 degrees below zero. Several of our church members related that they would come upon him hitch-hiking and stop to give him a ride. When he saw who they were, he would tell them to go on. He wanted to ride with some unsaved person he could tell about Christ. Mark was my youth pastor for three years. With him experiencing and practicing the Spirit-filled life, you will not be surprised that he has gone on to be Youth Pastor of some of America's largest and greatest churches. Mark now has a world-wide evangelistic ministry. The Spirit-filled life is the fruit bearing life.

THE FRUIT BEARING LIFE

"The fruit of the Spirit is love, joy, peace, longsuffering, goodness, gentleness, meekness, faith and self control." (Gal. 5:22-23.) Note that the word "fruit" here is singular. It is not "fruits" as plural, or nine different fruits. It is singular as one fruit. The nine facets of the fruit of the Spirit are just that, one fruit but nine facets of the character of the Spirit and of Christ.

Note also that it is the fruit of the Spirit, not the fruit of a Christian. It is the fruit of the Spirit who is given free reign of the Christian's life. It is the fruit of the Spirit manifested in the Christian's life. Every born again believer possesses the Holy Spirit. He possesses or has all of the Spirit. When you are saved the Spirit of Christ comes to live in you. You are sealed with the Holy Spirit unto the day of redemption. Eph. 1:13-14. You have all of Him, but does He have all of you? Unless the Holy Spirit has all of you He is not free to produce His fruit in you.

For many years I tried to produce the fruit of the Spirit in my life. I was determined that I would manifest all of the fruit of the Spirit by my will power and determination. To me, bearing the fruit of the Spirit was sort of like climbing a mountain. By my own strength and will I put forth all my efforts. It seemed sometimes as if after climbing so hard for days or weeks that I was about to reach the top. But when I least expected it I lost my hold and slipped all the way to the bottom. The end result of my continual effort to do so was frustration and discouragement.

It is no more difficult for the Spirit to produce patience in an impatient person, than a patient person. It is no problem for the Holy Spirit to produce love, joy, and peace in a person whose natural tendency is just the opposite. Our part in the fruit of the Spirit being produced in our life is our surrender to Him. Just let Him do His thing in your life. Jesus said, "for without me you can do nothing." (John 15:5.)

This certainly applies to bearing the fruit of the Spirit. Jesus said that to abide in the vine is to bear fruit, more fruit, and much fruit.

Also, the fruit of a Christian is another Christian. Spirit filled believers have God's power to help others come to Christ.

The Spirit-filled believer will experience victory in his life.

THE VICTORIOUS LIFE

It seems to me that most Christians live defeated and disappointed lives. They don't understand the scriptures. The meat of the Word makes them sick. They don't get "yes answers" to their prayers so they don't pray. They fall into all kinds of sin repeatedly. Jesus Christ is not real to them beyond an historic figure. The devil seems to be able to wallow them in his mud hole anytime he chooses. They have little love for God and His people, and no joy of the Lord, nor the peace of God that passes all understanding. Why is this so?

Jesus said that He "came that we might have life and have it more abundantly." (John 10:10b)

I believe the problem is that so many Christians walk in the flesh and live in the flesh which is contrary to walking in the Spirit. They try to do all their activities in their own power, and they fail every time. When Christ died on the cross, He defeated Satan, and overcame him. He destroyed the devil and his power of death. If we abide in Christ and are filled with the Spirit, we too are victorious over Satan. Jesus has already won the victory. It is our birthright to live in the victory that Christ won on the cross.

"Now thanks be unto God that always causes us to triumph in Christ." (2 Cor. 2:14.)

I thank God for that wonderful truth. If we live defeated lives, it indicates that we are not abiding in Christ, for in Him we always triumph. Sometimes the triumph may come differently than we expected. But we can always trust God to give us the victory in the ways that are best for us.

The Spirit-filled believer will experience answers to prayer.

ANSWERED PRAYER

The Spirit filled person always has his prayers answered. " If ye abide in me, and my words abide in you, ye shall ask what ye will, and it shall be done unto you. [8] Herein is my Father glorified, that ye bear much fruit; so shall ye be my disciples." (John 15:7-8)

The Spirit-filled person is first and foremost committed and surrendered to God. God's will is the priority of his life. Therefore he always prays according to the will of God. Like Jesus, he says to God, "This is what I want, but if it is not good for me to have it, give me what I need." And every time we ask for something according to the will of God, we get it. "And this is the confidence that we have in him, that if we ask any thing according to his will, he heareth us: [15] And if we know that he hear us, whatsoever we ask, we know that we have the petitions that we desired of him." (1 John 5:14-15).

But Satan lies to us and suggests that God doesn't care for us, doesn't hear us, or is not able to give us what we ask. Don't believe him. Believe the Word and stand on the Word.

"Now unto him that is able to do exceeding abundantly above all that we ask or think, according to the power that worketh in us, [21] Unto him *be* glory in the church by Christ Jesus throughout all ages, world without end. Amen." (Eph 3:20-21)

The Spirit-filled believer has God's power in his life.

THE GOD EMPOWERED LIFE

Jesus said, "you shall receive power after the Holy Ghost has come upon you, and you shall be witnesses to me both in Jerusalem, Judea, Samaria, and unto the uttermost part of the world." (Acts 1:8.)

He also told His disciples to "tarry in Jerusalem until you are endued with power from on high." (Lk. 24:48-49)

I believe Jesus gives us the power of the Holy Spirit for three reasons. First, He fills us with the Holy Spirit so that we will have the power to witness boldly and successfully of Him and His saving power and grace. Secondly, He seals us in Himself by or with the Spirit Who is our earnest of salvation unto the day of redemption. Thirdly, He gives the Holy Spirit to us for power for living and to be conformed unto His own image. The fruit of the Spirit is the character of Christ. We are sanctified by the Spirit. (2 Thess. 2:13.)

To be sealed in Christ by the Holy Spirit is a similar action by the Spirit to any object being sealed by its owner for safe keeping. It means we are safe in Jesus having been sealed there by God through His Spirit. "In whom ye also *trusted*, after that ye heard the word of truth, the gospel of your salvation: in whom also after that ye believed, ye were sealed with that Holy Spirit of promise, [14] Which is the earnest of our inheritance until the redemption of the purchased possession, unto the praise of his glory. (Eph 1:13-14)

> *I believe that when we put our faith and trust in the person of God, repent of our sins and confess our sins to Him, He forgives and cleanses us by the blood of Jesus Christ His Son. He seals us into Christ for our security. Then if by faith we ask for His filling and expect to be filled, we can then go in confidence that the power of God is upon us and with us.*

I believe the major reason so many believers are so shallow in the Word is they are not experiencing and walking in the Spirit filled life.

In 1 Cor. 2:9 and following we are told that "eye hath not seen, neither ear heard, nor has there entered in the heart of man, the things that God has prepared for them that love Him."

While this may include heaven which Jesus has gone to prepare for us, it includes much more. It includes the entire scope of the gospel and the inheritance of the child of God. It includes all the spiritual blessings God has blessed us with in Christ. It includes all God can and has provided for us in Jesus Christ. It includes all the mysteries of the gospel.

In 1 Cor. 2:10 the Word says, "But God hath revealed them unto us by His Spirit, for the Spirit searches all things, yea, the deep things of God."

When one is filled with the Spirit, the Word of God comes alive to them as rapidly as they can receive it and practice it. Of course, when we don't practice what we have received, we are in disobedience and rebellion and are no longer filled with the Holy Spirit. We have grieved Him and quenched Him. The Spirit reveals to us, and in us, the truth about the Lord Jesus Christ and makes Him very real to us. Oh, the blessings of being filled with and walking in the Holy Spirit.

DIFFERENT TERMS AND PHRASES USED IN THE NEW TESTAMENT TO DESCRIBE THE FILLING OF THE HOLY SPIRIT.

There are many different words and phrases used in the New Testament to describe the outpouring or filling with the Holy Spirit. The following list is not exhaustive by any means, but is revealing.

1. Baptized with the Holy Ghost. Mark 1:8; Acts 1:5, 11:16
2. Filled with the Holy Ghost. Acts 4:31
3. The Holy Ghost fell on them. Acts 10:44
4. The gift of the Holy Ghost was poured out . Acts 10:45
5. Receive the Holy Ghost. Acts 8:15
6. The Holy Ghost came on them. Acts 19:6
7. Gift of the Holy Ghost. Acts 11:7, and 2:38
8. The promise of my Father. Acts 1:4
9. Endued with power from on high. Lk. 24:48 ff.
10. Filled with all the fullness of God. Eph. 3:19
11. The power of His resurrection. Phil. 3:10 and Eph. 1:19-20
12. Anointed with the Holy Spirit and with power. Acts 10:38
13. He ...which anointed us is God. 2 Cor. 1:21
14. He was a good man and full of the Holy Ghost. Acts 11:24
15. I will put my Spirit upon Him. Matt. 12:18
16. The Spirit of God, like a dove, descending upon Him . Mark 1:10

The Spirit-filled life is a reality. It is much more than just being saved. It is God's provision for you to live on the highest plane. He tells us about the Spirit-filled life in His Word. He tells us how to be filled. He commands us to be filled. He shares with us the results of such a life. Why aren't more of us filled?

Since you are a believer, why not be filled with the Holy Spirit? Happy filling!

Chapter 2

Abundant Life in the Midst of Poverty

In the previous chapter, one of the characteristics of the Spirit-filled life was the abundant life. In this chapter we will see an example of a person who lived the abundant life in the midst of poverty everywhere else.

The Bible gives an account of a severe drought in Israel. The drought was the judgment of God upon His people for their wickedness. As a result of the drought, there was dearth, death, despair, and defeat on every hand.

"And Elijah the Tishbite, who was of the inhabitants of Gilead, said unto Ahab, As the LORD God of Israel liveth, before whom I stand, there shall not be dew nor rain these years, but according to my word. 2 And the word of the LORD came unto him, saying, 3 Get thee hence, and turn thee eastward, and hide thyself by the brook Cherith, that is before Jordan. 4 And it shall be, that thou shalt drink of the brook; and I have commanded the ravens to feed thee there. 5 So he went and did according unto the word of the LORD: for he went and dwelt by the brook Cherith, that is before Jordan. 6 And the ravens brought him bread and flesh in the morning, and bread and flesh in the evening; and he drank of the brook. 7 And it came to pass after a-while, that the brook dried up, because there had been no rain in the land. 8 And the word of the LORD came unto him, saying, 9 Arise, get thee to Zarephath, which belongeth to Zidon, and dwell there: behold, I have commanded a widow woman there to sustain thee. 10 So he arose and went to Zarephath. And when he came to the gate of the city, behold, the widow woman was there gathering of sticks: and he called to her, and said, Fetch me, I pray thee, a little water in a vessel, that I may drink. 11 And as she was going to fetch it, he called to her, and said,

Bring me, I pray thee, a morsel of bread in thine hand. 12 And she said, As the LORD thy God liveth, I have not a cake, but an handful of meal in a barrel, and a little oil in a cruse: and, behold, I am gathering two sticks, that I may go in and dress it for me and my son, that we may eat it, and die. 13 And Elijah said unto her, Fear not; go and do as thou hast said: but make me thereof a little cake first, and bring it unto me, and after make for thee and for thy son. 14 For thus saith the LORD God of Israel, The barrel of meal shall not waste, neither shall the cruse of oil fail, until the day that the LORD sendeth rain upon the earth. 15 And she went and did according to the saying of Elijah: and she, and he, and her house, did eat many days. 16 And the barrel of meal wasted not, neither did the cruse of oil fail, according to the word of the LORD, which he spake by Elijah." (1 Kings 17:1-16)

The drought and famine were so bad that Ahab, the King of Israel, sent men all over Israel and to other nations looking for Elijah. Ahab thought that the drought was because Elijah had prayed that it not rain in Israel until he said for it to. Elijah had told Ahab that he had so prayed, and Ahab mistakenly blamed Elijah for the drought rather than understanding that Elijah called for no rain because of Ahab's and Israel's sin.

One of the truths of this account is that Elijah fared sumptuously, abundantly, in the very midst of the poverty around him.

There is a spiritual drought in so many of our churches today. I do not find many "rivers of living water" flowing there. There seems a state of spiritual poverty in our midst. And what makes it so sad is the fact that our people either don't know it or are satisfied to live in this spiritual poverty. There seems to be very little difference in the way our people live and those on the outside of the church. In this chapter we will see how Elijah lives an abundant life while others all around him are starving.

In this account of Elijah and Ahab, there are six things involved in Elijah's abundant living.

1. THE WORD OF GOD

There can be no abundant life apart from the Word of God. God is the source of abundant life in the believer. His Word not only reveals the abundant life, which Jesus came to provide, (John10:10b), but it also teaches us how to experience it. Just like the Word of God reveals to us how to have life, it does the same for abundant life.

The Word of God reveals and relates to us the Person of God, and what kind of God He is. As we read and study the Word of God, we learn that God is a loving God Who wants His people to have the very best. He wants to "give us all things richly to enjoy." He wants us to be victorious over Satan's wiles, and to overcome the world's influence in our lives. The Word reveals that God stands ready to make His people experience life at its best for those who trust and obey Him.

The Word of God shows us God's purpose in our life. God saved us according to an eternal purpose.

" God; ⁹ Who hath saved us, and called *us* with an holy calling, not according to our works, but according to his own purpose and grace, which was given us in Christ Jesus before the world began," (2 Tim 1:8-9) Also, "And we know that all things work together for good to them that love God, to them who are the called according to *his* purpose." (Romans 8:28)

We can rest assured that it was not the purpose of God for us to live defeated lives all the time. The whole warp and woof of the Bible is about being victorious and the overcoming life.

The Word of God reveals to us the promises of God. "According as his divine power hath given unto us all things that *pertain* unto life and godliness, through the knowledge of him that hath called us to glory and virtue: ⁴ Whereby are given unto us exceeding great and precious promises: that by these ye might be partakers of the divine nature, having escaped the corruption that is in the world through lust." (2 Peter 1:3-4)

All of us would enjoy experiencing the blessings of God, without the laborious study of the Bible. But that is what is required to know what His promises are and to have the faith to claim them.

"Faith comes by hearing, and hearing by the Word of God." (Rom. 10:17.)

There are over 2,000 promises of God in the Bible. How many of them do we know about and trust God to provide for us?

The Word of God releases the power of God. When I read the Word of God I learn of His promises. When I believe the Word I've read, through the faith derived from study of the Word, I am preparing to make it mine. When I confess the Word through faith, it releases the power of God in my life to make the promise of God come to be in me. Elijah knew what God had said and believed it enough to act upon it.

2. Unquestioned Obedience To The Word Of God

To not question the Bible is not biblical idolatry. It is not Bible worship as some claim. It is an act of worship of Almighty God to believe His Word. It is the main source from which God speaks to us. Elijah obeyed what God said to him.

Elijah went and did according to God's Word even though it must have seemed unreasonable and impossible. It does not seem reasonable that ravens would feed a human being. Just the opposite would be expected. But God had said, "I have commanded the ravens to feed you there." v.4 The Bible teaches us to be doers of the Word, not just hearers. Elijah was a doer as well as a hearer. One must hear before he can do what God says.

Our Lord Jesus Christ made some pretty wonderful promises to those who keep His commandments. In John 14:21,23 He said, "He that hath my commandments, and keepeth them, he it is that loveth me; and he that loveth me shall be loved of my Father, and I will love him and manifest myself unto him.....If a man love me he will keep my words, and my Father will love him, and we will come unto him, and make our abode with him."

Jesus' promise was to them that obeyed His word. Obedience is absolutely imperative for Jesus to manifest Himself to us, and for Him and the Father to love us and come to abide with us. I think that Jesus is talking about abiding with us in all the fullness of the Godhead bodily.

God encourages us to be obedient. Joshua 1:7-8 tells us to "observe to do." In Acts 5:32. He promised the Holy Spirit to those that "obeyed Him." The first and greatest command of God to His people is to love Him with all that we are and have. This begins with obedience. Perhaps the Bible has more to say about loving and obeying God than any other one thing.

In obedience to the Word of God, Elijah saw the hand of God move on his behalf. He obeyed in going to the brook Cherith and the ravens fed him there, but only there. He obeyed and went to the widow of Zarephath, and God made the barrel of flour and cruse of oil last until the famine was over. If Elijah had gone to any other place than the brook Cherith, or the widow of Zarephath, I doubt he would have been fed. He obeyed the Word of God explicitly and saw God's hand on his behalf.

Disobedience, in whole or in part, will deny us the blessings that God wants to give us. Dr. Stephen Olford used to say that partial obedience was in fact total disobedience. A good example of this is king Saul in 1 Samuel 15:22. He did what God told him, except for what he thought was not wise nor necessary. Because of it he lost his kingdom. In what way do we lose by partial or total disobedience?

Too many of us treat the Word of God as we do the food in a cafeteria line. We go down the line looking at each item, and choosing only what appeals to us. Or we already have our minds made up as to what appeals to us and totally ignore the rest. Are not we guilty of doing the same thing with the Word of God that Saul did? All of the Bible is the Word of God, not just what appeals to us. Obedience is an absolute if we are to be filled with and walk in the Spirit.

3. Elijah Expected God To Keep His Word

In obedience to God's Word, Elijah went to the brook Cherith. He went expecting God to feed him by the ravens. He went to Zarephath expecting God to care for him through the widow, not because it was the most likely place to be fed, but because God said He had commanded her to. He expected God to work. Even when the widow told him she was gathering two sticks of wood to cook the last mouthful of food she had, Elijah expected God to work. He instructed her to prepare and bring to him bread and water before she fed her son and herself.

How did God respond to Elijah's obedience and expectation? He performed a miracle to provide for them all as long as the famine lasted. The flour in the barrel and the oil in the cruse did not fail. They had sufficient to eat every day.

How will God respond to us when we believe, obey, and expect Him to fill us with His Spirit? You can take it to the bank. He will keep His Word. Jesus told the two blind men in Matt. 9:29 who had asked Him for mercy, "As your faith is so be it unto you." They believed, they expected, and they were healed of blindness.

4. Elijah Was Undaunted By The Obstacles

There was inadequate food even for the family, much less Elijah. The widow swore that she was preparing the very last of any food in the house. But this did not faze Elijah. Had not God promised? Would not God keep His Word? Elijah did not believe this obstacle would or could hinder God. He immediately instructed her to cook and bring him a cake first.

Another obstacle was the negative attitude of the widow "that we may eat it and die."

The church is full of negative attitudes. Every way you turn, someone is telling you it can't be done. We have never done it that way before. Don't be too enthused. Don't expect too much. You'll be disappointed. Elijah did not let the negative attitude of the widow dull his faith that God would do exactly as He had said. We need to trust God rather than look at the obstacles. Then too:

5. Elijah Put God's Word Above The Circumstances

Most of the time in our lives, circumstances do not seem favorable, or are not favorable to God's promises being fulfilled. Elijah could have let fear of the widow's circumstances keep him from telling her to bring him food before she and her son ate. But God had told him that He had commanded this widow to feed him. He trusted God's Word more than he feared the circumstances. There was a famine in the land that extended to Zarephath of Sidon. How could the widow possibly feed him? She couldn't even feed herself and her son. But God had commanded the widow to do so, and Elijah trusted Him.

6. Elijah Enjoyed The Victory Of Abundant Living

After he had heard the Word of God, after he had obeyed the Word of God, after he expected God to keep His Word and work on his behalf, after he refused to be discouraged by the obstacles and circumstances, Elijah enjoyed the victory. What God had promised to him God had done. They all ate sufficiently throughout the famine. We can live victorious lives, as individuals, even if all around us others are not. Even in the midst of defeat and God's judgment, we can enjoy the abundant life.

"Trust in the Lord with all thine heart, and lean not unto your own understanding, but in all thy ways acknowledge Him and He shall direct your paths.". (Prov. 3:5-6.)

How would you rate your life as to abundant living? Are you experiencing and enjoying the abundant life? Do you see yourself and those around you in spiritual poverty? Is there a desire to have a glorious exit from it? You can exit the spiritual poverty around you and within you by being filled with the Holy Spirit.

Since you are a believer, why **not** be filled with the Holy Spirit? Happy abundant living!!!

Chapter 3

The Fact of the Spirit Filled Life

The filling of the Holy Spirit is a real event, both in the Old Testament and the New. It is also a fact that the Holy Spirit worked differently with people in the Old Testament than in the New. In the Old Testament, the Spirit of God normally came and went on men as it suited the purpose of God for that man. The exception to that rule seems to be David whom we will deal with later.

In the New Testament, when a person is born again, (born again is the term used by Jesus to identify the spiritual birth one experiences in becoming a Christian), the Holy Spirit comes to seal (the sealing of the Holy Spirit of a Christian into Christ is the act of securing that person to be in Christ for life), and dwell in him as long as he lives on this earth.

He "never leaves them nor forsakes them." (Heb. 13: 5.) Repeatedly, we are told in the New Testament that we are indwelt by the Holy Spirit. "If any man has not the Spirit of Christ, he is none of His." (Rom. 8:9b.) So the Holy Spirit comes to take abode in the believer's life at the time He gives the spiritual birth to him.

And all of the Spirit comes to dwell in the believer. The Holy Spirit is a Person. He is equal in essence with the Father and the Son. He is referred to as the Spirit of God, the Spirit of Christ, the Holy Spirit, and the Spirit. When He comes in to dwell He comes in His entirety. God doesn't give you a little bit of His Spirit today and more tomorrow. So every believer possesses the person of the Holy Spirit from the day of his spiritual birth.

MAKE HIM PRESIDENT

Unfortunately, the Holy Spirit does not possess all of us. Too many of us restrict the Holy Spirit to certain areas of our life. We need to let Him have control over every area of our life. As has been said, the Holy Spirit is Resident in every believer's life. But each believer has to make Him President. The Holy Spirit will not force Himself on us in His fullness. It is up to us to seek Him through Jesus. It is possible for a believer to be saved and filled with the Holy Spirit at the same time. This results in a big difference in the new believer. Though his capacity for filling is very small, nevertheless that capacity is filled.

SUBSEQUENT TO THE NEW BIRTH

The New Testament seems to teach that the filling of the Holy Spirit, or the pouring out of the Spirit, is an experience in addition to and subsequent to the new birth. This whole chapter will seek to demonstrate that truth.

Let me illustrate. A man may take a double barreled shotgun with both barrels loaded. He pulls both triggers exactly simultaneously and only an expert knows that there were two experiences or explosions taking place. But he may take the same loaded shotgun and pull the trigger of one barrel now and the second 10 minutes or 10 years later and everyone knows that there were two explosions. It is the same way with being saved and being filled with the Holy Spirit. A person may be saved and filled with the Spirit seemingly at the same time. The average believer would think that "he just got saved good" and not realize that they were filled as well as saved. The Spirit-filled believer would recognize the difference from the fruit of the Spirit in his life, and know that he was filled as well as saved. On the other hand, a person may be saved at one time and filled much later. Then everyone can recognize the person has had two experiences. The person who is filled simultaneously with being saved grows and develops more rapidly than the other who is saved only. But it takes "an expert", one that understands the Spirit-filled life, to tell that he was saved and filled.

We often wonder why one believer grows so rapidly and another so slowly. It is because the first was filled with the Spirit when he was saved, and the second was not. I do not see these two events or experiences as a first and second blessing. A person is born again only once. His new birth is good forever. But a person needs to be filled with the Holy Spirit many, many times. One filling is not sufficient. This is true because we "leak". Neither are we "so sanctified" that we never sin again. Every time we sin, we need to repent, confess and be filled anew.

Some Old Testament Believers Were Filled With The Spirit.

1. Joshua was a man full of the Holy Spirit. God transferred to Joshua the honor that was on Moses. (Num. 27:15-23.) Joshua was filled with the Holy Spirit by the laying on of Moses' hands. (Deut. 34:9)

2. David was a Spirit-filled man. God chose David above all his brothers to be the next king of Israel. (1 Samuel 16:3-7.) Then God had Samuel anoint David with oil and the Bible says that "the Spirit came upon him from that day forward." (1 Sam. 16:13)

3. I take that statement to mean that the Spirit came on David for the rest of his life. This was not a sure thing for others. The very next verse tells us that the Spirit of the Lord departed from Saul. David was certainly used of God for the rest of his life in spite of his sins, or maybe because of them. In the Psalms, David taught us many lessons that he learned from his sins.

4. Isaiah was anointed and filled with the Holy Spirit, Well spake the Holy Ghost by Esaias the prophet unto our fathers, (Acts 28:25) When Isaiah said, "the Spirit of the Lord is upon me", we know that it was a prophecy about Jesus. But Isaiah may have talking about himself as well.

God also lets us know that His Spirit, or the Spirit of Christ, was upon the Old Testament prophets when they were prophesying. In 1 Pet. 1:10-11 we read, "Of which salvation the prophets have inquired and searched diligently , searching what or what manner of time the Spirit of Christ, which was in them did signify…." And in 2 Peter 1:21 "For the prophecy came not in old time by the will of man, but holy men of God spoke as they were moved by the Holy Ghost."

There seems to be more than ample evidence that the Holy Spirit of God was upon the Old Testament prophets to enable them to function as God willed.

NEW TESTAMENT CHRISTIANS WERE ALSO FILLED WITH THE HOLY SPIRIT

It is a fact that many or most of the early New Testament believers were filled for service. While the Spirit never left them, there were repeated fillings of the same people.

In Eph. 5:18 God commands us, " And be not drunk with wine wherein is excess, but be filled with the Spirit"…it really says be you being filled. This infers many fillings. It certainly would be nice if a believer in the Lord could be filled one time and never have to repeat. But we are human. Some of us sin very often. Sin breaks our fellowship with God, not our relationship in the truest sense of the word, but our fellowship. We are then no longer filled. To be filled, we must repent, confess and asked to be filled again. The late Bill Bright, president of Campus Crusade for Christ, used to say that it was something like breathing. We breathe out carbon dioxide and breathe in oxygen. Likewise the Spirit filled believer breathes in the Holy Spirit and breathes out sin by repenting and being filled. Some New Testament examples of filling are:

1. John the Baptist. John the Baptist is the first person in the New Testament to be specified as being filled with the Holy Spirit. And his filling was different from all others. John the Baptist was filled with the Holy Spirit from his mother's womb. (Luke 1:15) This may be referring to the time when Mary visited Elizabeth and upon her salutation to Elizabeth, the babe leaped in Elizabeth's womb.
2. Our Lord Jesus Was filled with the Holy Spirit.

    In Acts 10:38 it says, "you know…how God anointed Jesus of Nazareth with the Holy Ghost and power, who went about doing good…." When was Jesus so anointed? Luke tells us in 3:21-22 "Now when all the people were baptized, it came to pass, that Jesus also being baptized, and praying, the heavens opened, and the Holy Ghost descended in bodily shape like a dove upon Him, and a voice came from heaven, which said, Thou art my beloved Son, in Thee I am well pleased."

Note that from verse 23 to verse 38 in Luke 3, the genealogy of Jesus is given.

Then in Luke 4:1 it says, "And Jesus being full of the Holy Spirit, returned from Jordan and was led by the Spirit into the wilderness." Verses 4:2 through 13 tell about Jesus' temptation. In verse 14 we are told, "And Jesus returned in the power of the Spirit into Galilee, and there went out a fame of Him in all the region round about."

Jesus' filling with the Holy Spirit was also different. Because He never sinned and always did those things that pleased the Father, He never needed to be filled again. But it is a fact of scripture that He was filled.

3. The apostles were filled with the Holy Spirit. In Acts 1:5 we read, "For John truly baptized with water, but you shall be baptized with the Holy Ghost not many days hence."

It seems to me that Peter was saved before Pentecost. In Matt. 16:16, Peter made a profession of faith equal to anyone believing in Jesus for salvation when he testified, "Thou are the Christ, the Son of the living God."

In Acts 2:4 ff the apostles were filled with the Holy Spirit. Some of the same apostles, including Peter, were filled again in Acts 4:8 and 30-31.

4. Paul was filled with the Holy Spirit. Paul met Jesus on the Damascus Road and surrendered to Him as Lord. Every scholar that I have read counts Paul's conversion at his experience on the Damascus Road. Paul was blinded and had to be led into Damascus. Three days later God sent Ananias to Paul so that "you might receive your sight and be filled with the Holy Spirit." (Acts 9"17) Note again that there was time between his salvation and his first filling. Some argue that God was gradually working out His plan. But God is the same always. I believe that Peter and Paul were saved and filled the same way I was almost 2,000 years later.

5. Barnabas was full of the Holy Spirit, and served God effectively. (Acts 11:24.)

THE EARLY CHURCH WAS FILLED

1. The church at Samaria that was formed under Phillip's preaching
    was filled. "But when they believed Phillip's preaching the
    things concerning the kingdom of God, and the Name of Jesus
    Christ, they were baptized, both men and women." (Acts 8:12.)
    Phillip was filled with the Spirit and performed many miracles.
    Would this Spirit filled man have baptized unbelievers? I think not.
    Yet when the word got back to the church in Jerusalem, they sent
    Peter and John to Samaria.

    Now how long it took the word to get back to Jerusalem is not
    known. It was certainly some bit of time. And it took Peter and
    John some more time to reach Samaria. The very first thing that
    the two from Jerusalem did was to pray for the saved Samaritans,
    that they receive the Holy Spirit. A thing of note here is that the
    word "receive" is in the active voice. Normally the word receive is
    in the passive voice because the object receives the action. Because
    it is in the active voice, it means that the Samaritans were to take
    the initiative in receiving the Holy Spirit. They were to reach
    out by faith and "take" the Holy Spirit. Then the apostles from
    Jerusalem laid hands on them and they received the Holy Spirit.

    Now there was such a difference in the Samaritan believers that
    when Simon the Sorcerer saw that through the laying on of the
    apostles' hands the Holy Spirit was given, he offered them money for
    the same power. One of the points that I want to make here is that
    there was such a difference in the Samaritan believers immediately
    following their filling, that Simon the Sorcerer noticed it and wanted
    to be able to do the same to others, no doubt for the wrong reasons.

    The second point I want to call to your attention is that the Holy
    Spirit was imparted at the laying on of the apostles' hands. Remember
    that the same thing was true of Paul. When Ananias laid hands on
    Paul, he received the Holy Spirit. Later Paul laid hands on some
    disciples in Ephesus and they received the Holy Spirit. (Acts 19:1-7)

2. The church at Caesarea was filled also. In Acts 10, Peter had been
    sent to Caesarea by a vision from God and a request from Cornelius.
    Peter went and preached Jesus unto them. "While Peter yet spoke
    these words, the Holy Ghost fell on all of them which heard the
    word." (Acts 10:44.) The Jews that were with Peter, like some of us,

were surprised that the Holy Spirit was poured out on the Gentiles. Then Peter had them baptized.

When Peter returned to Jerusalem, the legalistic believers contended with him because he had baptized Gentiles also. Then Peter did a very wise thing, and something we could learn to our benefit. He rehearsed the matter from the beginning. He did this instead of defending himself. Good communications and explanations solve so many of our problems as they did his.

Part of the rehearsal was, "And as I began to speak the Holy Ghost fell on them as on us at the beginning. Then remembered I the word of the Lord, how that He said, John indeed baptized with water; but you shall be baptized with the Holy Ghost" (Acts 11:15-16.)

Peter just told them that he could not argue with God. It may be of interest to you that here it seems that Peter equated the "baptism of the Holy Spirit" with the initial filling of the Holy Spirit, or the Holy Spirit falling on all them which heard the Word.

3. The church in Antioch of Pisidia also demonstrates the fact of the filling of the Holy Spirit. When Paul and Barnabas turned to the Gentiles because of the opposition from the Jews over many conversions, the Jews were incensed and began to make trouble and persecute the believers. They expelled Paul and Barnabas who shook the dust off their feet against them. "And the disciples were filled with joy and the Holy Ghost." (Acts 13: 52.)

4. Paul later went to Ephesus. There he found certain disciples whom he asked, "Have you received the Holy Ghost since you believed?" (Acts 19:2) When Paul heard their answer, he asked, "Unto what then were you baptized? And they said, unto John's baptism. Then said Paul, John verily baptized with the baptism of repentance, saying unto the people, that they should believe on Him that should come after him, that is, on Christ Jesus. When they heard this, they were baptized in the Name of the Lord Jesus." (Acts 19:2-5.)

Now I would have a hard time believing that the apostle Paul would baptize a person whom he did not believe was saved. Sometime after he had baptized the 12, whether 30 minutes or 3 days, "And when Paul had laid his hands upon them, The Holy Ghost came on them; and they spoke with tongues and prophesied." (Acts 19:6.) There was some time between their salvation experience and baptism, and when the Holy Spirit came on them after Paul laid hands on them. It appears that the evidence is that a person may be, but is not necessarily filled with the Holy Spirit at the same time that they are saved.

MY OWN EXPERIENCE

In my own experience, the first filling came five months after I was wonderfully saved. With my wife, it was seventeen years after being saved. And what a difference it made in our lives. We were now on the same spiritual wave length. My daughter was filled 12 years after being saved. And yet, some people are filled at the same time they are saved. How fortunate!

In my own experience I was filled at the conclusion of a worship service. I had an overwhelming thirst for God and His Son Jesus. Of course, I have been filled countless times since then. Like others, I leak. One filling is not sufficient for all of life. When I have sinned, I have confessed that sin immediately and asked to be filled again.

My wife and children had different experiences than I had, but the change was just as real. I hesitated to give my experience lest others think they must have a similar one. Mine was unique. I have seen hundreds of others filled with similar results whose experience was nothing like mine.

I immediately began to study the Bible on the subject of being filled and was able to see the reality and biblical truth of being filled.

But the important issue is, not WHEN you were filled, but HAVE you been. And are you being filled and refilled so that you are walking in the Spirit? There is a marked difference in a believer who has been filled and one who has not. On the day of Pentecost the disciples were filled and the critics thought they were drunk.. In Acts 4:8 Peter and John were filled and the Jews "took knowledge that they had been with Jesus."

In Acts 4:30-31 they were filled and spoke the Word of God with boldness, and with great power they gave witness to the resurrection of Jesus. In Acts 8, there was such a difference that Simon wanted to buy the ability to cause others to be filled. In Acts 10, the Holy Spirit fell on them and they spoke with tongues and magnified God. In Acts 13, they were filled with joy. In Acts 19, they spoke with tongues and prophesied. In Ephesians 5:18-25, God commanded them to be filled long after becoming believers and showed them in the verses following verse 18 what a Spirit filled believer looked like.

A BRIEF WORD ABOUT TONGUES

Just a very brief word about tongues and the filling of the Holy Spirit. On two different occasions the filled people spoke in tongues in the New Testament. But more didn't than did. From the biblical perspective, tongues are not a language that any person can understand. Tongues are not a human language. Only God understand them and they are designed for the purpose of communicating with Him. I have never spoken in tongues and have no need or desire to. I have preached many, many revivals and Bible Conferences on the Spirit-filled Life, as well as led seminars on the same, and of all the people who were filled, I don't know of any that spoke in tongues immediately, though a few did later on. But if God chooses to give you the gift of tongues, praise Him, for God gives nothing that is not good!!!

Tongues are not always the evidence of filling. It may be for those to whom God gives the gift of speaking in a language no one understands, for they speak to God and not to man. (1 Cor.14:2)

The Spirit-filled life is a Biblical fact, of both New and Old Testaments. Let me encourage you to take God's Word for it rather than the word of man. Search the scriptures and you will know the truth, which will set you free to be filled.

Since you are a believer, why not be filled with the Holy Spirit? Happy filling!!!!

Chapter 4

The Need for the Spirit Filled Life

As we read about the Spirit-filled believers in the book of Acts, multitudes of people were saved at the preaching of the Word. (Acts 2:41.) People were being saved daily and added to the church.

(Acts 2:47.) "And believers were the more added to the Lord, multitudes both of men and women." (Acts 5:14) "Then had the churches rest throughout all Judea, and Galilee, and Samaria, and were edified:" "and walking in the fear of the Lord and the comfort of the Holy Ghost, were multiplied." (Acts 9:31.)

In view of the results of the preaching of the word in Acts by Spirit-filled preachers, why, in one of America's most evangelistic denominations, does it take about 40 people one year to persuade one person to be baptized? One baptism for every 40 members includes the baptism of the church members' children. It seems to me that something is terribly wrong or ineffective. We have all the modern conveniences and technologies to assist us in the proclamation of the Word, but with little effect. Thousands of churches go without one baptism in a whole year while the number of people needing to know Christ increases daily. In the same denomination that it took 40 persons to baptize one person in a year, there were 10,000 churches that did not baptize one person all year.

WHY?

Why is it that some believers read the Bible and have little understanding of it? Why do so many believers not believe that God answers prayer? Why are so many believers afraid to give witness of what Jesus has done in their lives? We witness about our new home, our new car, and our new clothes, but we are afraid to witness about our new life in Christ.

Many of us are like the apostles in the upper room before Pentecost, who were afraid of the Jews. We are afraid of everyone. The apostles changed drastically after their Pentecost filling with the Holy Spirit. They were very bold in the presence of the same Jews, and the results were fantastic. What made the difference? Just this, the filling of the Holy Spirit.

I believe that the greatest need in the church today is the power of God on us for service, and for living. We need to be filled with the Holy Spirit. God said to the saints at Ephesus, "Be filled with the Spirit." (Eph. 5:18.) (Or, be being filled with the Spirit.) Being filled with the Spirit is not a one time thing. We need to be filled often for every act of service and for every hour of our living.

The goals of this chapter are to help us see the need for all the church being filled with the Holy Spirit, and especially ourselves. I have found it to be a very profitable thing to ask God to fill me with His Spirit each time I go to the pulpit to preach or teach. I also ask for filling at every chance to witness, comfort, and counsel. If you are not being filled with the power of God for service and living, my prayer is that you will be moved to see your need and move to meet it.

As we deal with the need to be filled, it automatically follows that it is necessary to repeat some of the same scriptures, experiences, and persons that were cited in the chapter on the fact of the Spirit filled life. The application will be different.

THE OLD TESTAMENT PROPHETS NEEDED TO BE FILLED WITH THE SPIRIT.

DAVID

The prophet and king, David, needed to be filled with the Holy Spirit. 1 Sam.16:12-13. (David was a prophet as well as king. Acts 2:29-30) King Saul had messed up and God had told him that he could no longer be king. Then God chose David, son of Jesse, to be king. He sent the prophet Samuel down to Bethlehem to anoint David to be the next king. Being the youngest of Jesse's sons, he was in the field tending his father's sheep.

When God would not accept any of Jesse's other sons, they sent for David to come to Samuel. "And he sent and brought him in. Now he was ruddy and of a beautiful countenance, and goodly to look to. And the Lord said, Arise and anoint him, for this is he. Then Samuel took the horn of oil and anointed him in the midst of his brethren: and the Spirit of the Lord came upon David from that day forward...." (1 Sam. 16:12-13.)

The first thing that God did for David to enable him to serve was to anoint him with the Holy Spirit. David is unique in that, of all of the Old Testament prophets, he was the only one of which it is said that the Holy Spirit was upon him continually. This may be hard to understand in the light of what David did later. Why did not the Spirit depart from him as He did from Saul? I don't pretend to understand all of God's ways, but I do believe all of His Word. But the main point here is that David needed to be filled with the Holy Spirit.

MOSES AND JOSHUA

Moses and Joshua needed and experienced the Spirit-filled life. "And Moses spoke unto the Lord, saying, Let the Lord, the God of the spirits of all flesh, set a man over the congregation, which may go out before them, and which may go in before them, and which may lead them out, and which may lead them in; that the congregation of the Lord be not as sheep which have no shepherd.

And the Lord said unto Moses, "Take thee Joshua, the son of Nun, a man in whom is the Spirit, and lay thy hand upon him; and set him before Eleazer the priest, and before all the congregation, and give him a charge in their sight. And thou shalt put some of thine honor upon him, that all the congregation of the children of Israel may be obedient.........And he laid his hands upon him and gave him a charge, as the Lord commanded by the hand of Moses." (Num. 27:15-20, 23.)

"And Joshua the son of Nun was full of the Spirit of wisdom; for Moses had laid his hands upon him; and the children of Israel hearkened unto him, and did as the Lord commanded Moses." (Deut. 34: 9)

ISAIAH

What about Isaiah the prophet? Paul said of him, "Well spake the Holy Ghost by Isaiah the prophet...." (Acts 28:25)

It seems to me that all of God's prophets were filled with the Holy Spirit from time to time, especially as they wrote the scriptures. Later Peter tells us that "Knowing this first, that no prophecy of the scripture is of any private interpretation (origin), for the prophecy came not in old time by the will of man; but holy men of God spake as they were moved by the Holy Ghost." (2 Pet. 1:20-21.)

ALL OF THE PROPHETS

Peter also gives us even more evidence that the Old Testament prophets were filled with the Holy Spirit when they spoke. "Of which salvation the prophets have inquired and searched diligently, who prophesied of the grace that should come unto you; searching what or what manner of time the Spirit of Christ which was in them did signify, when it testified beforehand the sufferings of Christ and the glory that should follow." (1 Pet. 1:10-11.)

Peter seems to include all the prophets in these two references. The Spirit of Christ is another name by which the Spirit of God is called. The Spirit of Christ was in the prophets, directing their prophecy and writings.

Zechariah seemed to sum it all up when he said, "...Not by might, nor by power, but by my Spirit, saith the Lord of hosts." (Zech. 4:6.)

What a comfort it is to the child of God to know that every bit of the Word of God is God breathed. We don't have to use our own wisdom to determine which part of the Bible is God breathed and which part is not. I believe that it all is.

New Testament People Needed To Be Filled With The Spirit.

John The Baptist Needed To Be Filled

John the Baptist needed to be filled with the Holy Spirit. In Luke's gospel, verses 15 through16 it says, when the angel Gabriel came to announce the coming conception and birth of John the Baptist to Zacharias, "For he shall be great in the sight of the Lord, and shall drink neither wine nor strong drink; and he shall be filled with the Holy Ghost, even from his mother's womb. And many of the children of Israel shall he turn to the Lord their God." (Luke 1:15-16)

It is not said of any other of God's children that they were filled from their mother's womb. But I encourage you to take note that John the Baptist needed to be filled with the Holy Spirit in spite of the fact of being chosen by God for the special purpose of being the forerunner of Jesus. John the Baptist needed to be filled in spite of the fact that he was born of godly parents. He needed to be filled with the Spirit in spite of the fact that Gabriel announced his birth to Zacharias, even in spite of the fact that Jesus said that there were none greater than John the Baptist.

Jesus Needed To Be Filled

Jesus our Lord needed to be filled with the Holy Spirit. In Acts 10:38 God records for us, "You know.....how God anointed Jesus of Nazareth with the Holy Ghost and with power; who went about doing good, and healing all that were oppressed of the devil, for God was with him."

Where and when did God anoint Jesus? It happened at His baptism. In Luke 3:21-22, it is recorded that "Now when all the people were baptized, it came to pass, that Jesus also being baptized, and praying, the heaven was opened, and the Holy Ghost descended in bodily form like a dove upon him, and a voice came from heaven which said, Thou art my beloved Son; in thee I am well pleased."

The rest of that chapter records the genealogy of Jesus. And in Luke 4:1, it says, "And Jesus being full of the Holy Ghost returned from

Jordan, and was led by the Spirit into the wilderness." And in verses 14 and 15 of chapter 4, "And Jesus returned in the power of the Spirit into Galilee; and there went out a fame of him through all the region round about. And he taught in their synagogues, being glorified of all."

It really does amaze me---in fact it almost blows my mind---that Jesus needed to be filled with the Holy Spirit. But He did. He did in spite of the fact that He was the only begotten Son of God. He needed this filling in spite of the fact that He was conceived by the Holy Spirit and born of a virgin. He did in spite of the fact that He never sinned. He needed to be filled in spite of His pre-existence and His coming down from heaven. He needed to be filled because He was human as well as divine.

In the power of the Holy Spirit, He healed, raised some from the dead, preached the word, and saved all that trusted Him. In the power of the Spirit He resisted temptation, (Luke 4:2-13), died on the cross, (Heb. 9:14), and arose from the dead. (Romans 8:11.) If all the above is true, and it is, what about we poor mortals? How desperately we need God's power received by the fullness of the Spirit! Every time I read or think about my Lord needing to be filled with the Holy Spirit for His ministry, I feel like a spiritual pauper. I would despair if I did not know that the same Holy Spirit will fill me when I meet His conditions.

THE APOSTLES NEEDED TO BE FILLED

The apostles needed to be filled with the Holy Spirit. In Luke 24:45-49 is recorded the last instructions of Jesus to His apostles and disciples "Then opened he their understanding that they might understand the scriptures. And said unto them, thus it is written and thus it behooved Christ to suffer and to rise from the dead on the third day: And that repentance and remissions of sins should be preached in his name among all nations, beginning at Jerusalem. And ye are witnesses of these things. And behold, I send the promise of my Father upon you: but tarry ye in the city of Jerusalem until ye be endued with power from on high." (Luke 24:45-49)

"And being assembled together with them, commanded them that they should not depart from Jerusalem, but wait for the promise of the Father, which saith he, ye have heard of me. For John truly baptized with water; but ye shall be baptized with the Holy Ghost not many days hence.......And ye shall receive power after the Holy Ghost is come upon you, and ye shall be witnesses...." (Acts.1:4-5, 8.)

These apostles had been with Jesus for over three years. They had heard Him preach and teach. They had seen Him heal the sick and raise the dead. They had observed Him perform miracle after miracle. They had even been sent out to witness with power over demons. I believe that their learning and experiences with Jesus for three years was far superior to any seminary training we have today. You would have thought that they were well prepared. But Jesus told them to wait for the filling of the Holy Spirit, which took place the first time at Pentecost. I joy every time I read the book of Acts at what the Holy Spirit did through those He had filled, and I earnestly long to be so used.

The apostle Paul needed to be filled with the Holy Spirit. On his way to Damascus to arrest Christian believers, he met Jesus face to face, so to speak. Paul was blinded by the brightness and glory of Jesus as He appeared to him. Every scholar that I have read seems to believe that this is when Paul was converted to Christ. Being without sight, he was led by others to Damascus and was three days without sight.

Then God sent one of His disciples to Paul. "And Ananias went his way, and entered into the house; and putting his hands on him said, Brother Saul, the Lord even Jesus, that appeared unto thee in the way as thou camest, hast sent me, that thou mightest receive thy sight and be filled with the Holy Ghost." (Acts 9:17.)

A casual reading of the book of Acts will reveal to the alert believer that these apostles needed and received repeated fillings. The apostle Paul arose, and after his baptism, he preached Jesus to those he had intended to arrest. He became one of God's greatest, but only after he was filled with the Holy Spirit. It seems to me that such testimony from the scriptures would reveal our need to us as well as to others.

THE EARLY CHURCH

The early church needed to be filled with the Holy Spirit. Thousands of men and women were converted to Christ under the preaching of the apostles and other believers. All of these thousands also needed to be filled. In Acts 4, we have the account of Peter and John being brought before the rulers and elders and scribes, and were threatened with arrest and punishment if they preached anymore about Jesus. "And being let go, they went to their own company...., And when they had prayed, the place was shaken where they were assembled together; and they were ALL filled with the Holy Ghost and spake the word of God with boldness." (Acts 4: 23, 31.)

Note that even though Peter was filled in Acts 2:4 and 4:8, he was among the "company" of those filled again in 4:31.

IN SAMARIA

In Acts 8, we find Phillip, one of the original seven deacons, had gone down to Samaria and was preaching the gospel.. He also was performing miracles, casting out demons and healing the sick, the palsied, and the lame. Verse 12 says, "But when they believed Phillip preaching the things concerning the kingdom of God, and the name of Jesus Christ, they were baptized, both men and women." We are told that they believed the preaching about the Kingdom of God and the name of Jesus Christ.

That is certainly what we "require" today for a man or woman to be saved. Then Phillip baptized them. It certainly doesn't seem that a Spirit-filled preacher would be baptizing unsaved people. I believe that Phillip was filled with the Spirit of God in order to do the things he was doing, healing, casting out demons, and miracles.

It is a certain thing that they received the Spirit, but not necessarily that they were filled with Him. For we are told in verses Acts 8:14-20 of their needing to be filled with the Holy Spirit and the fact that they were. When Peter and John came down from Jerusalem, they recognized immediately that these new believers had not been filled with the Spirit, so they prayed for them to be so. When Peter and John laid their hands on them, they were filled. The event and experience was so obvious that Simon, a converted scorcerer, offered money to Peter and John to give him the power to lay hands on people and they be filled. Of course, they refused.

IN EPHESUS

In Acts 19:1-7, Paul came to Ephesus and found 12 disciples in whom he did not recognize the Holy Spirit. When he asked them about the Spirit, they didn't know that the Holy Spirit was yet given, having been baptized unto John's baptism. Paul preached to them that they were to believe on Jesus. "When they heard this, they were baptized in the name of the Lord Jesus. And when Paul laid his hands on them, the Holy Ghost came on them...." (Acts 19: 5-6.)

It would not seem that Paul would baptize men whom he was not sure had trusted Christ. Yet sometime after baptism, he laid hands on them and they were filled with the Holy Spirit. Because these 12 spoke in tongues, some have mistakenly taught that all people filled must or would speak in tongues. While I believe that tongues is a valid spiritual gift today, in my many experiences of filling, I have never spoken in tongues.

When Paul wrote to the church at Ephesus sometime later, he gave them, and all believers, God's command to be filled with the Spirit."And be not drunk with wine wherein is excess, but be filled with the Spirit." (Eph. 5:18) Since this is a command, it naturally follows that believers who are not filled with the Spirit are in direct disobedience and are grieving the Holy Spirit, both of which are sin.

[18] And be not drunk with wine, wherein is excess; but be filled with the Spirit; [19] Speaking to yourselves in psalms and hymns and spiritual songs, singing and making melody in your heart to the Lord; [20] Giving thanks always for all things unto God and the Father in the name of our Lord Jesus Christ; [21] Submitting yourselves one to another in the fear of God. (Eph 5:18-21) A casual reading of the rest of chapters 5 and 6 of Ephesians, along with these verses would show what a Spirit filled believer acts like. When we measure ourselves by God's standard, do we fall short?

CONTEMPORARY LEADERS

Great Christians since have testified to being filled with the Spirit. Jonathan Edwards, John Wesley, Dwight L. Moody, Charles Finney, A.J. Gordon, Billy Sunday, Vance Havner, W.A. Criswell, Billy Graham, R.A. Torrey, Bill Bright, Charles Stanley and many, many more. It seems obvious, that in order to be effective in ministry, we need to be filled too!

THE CONTEMPORARY CHURCH NEEDS TO BE FILLED

We of the modern day church need to be filled with the Holy Spirit. We need to be filled first, because God commanded us to be. But there are many other obvious reasons including the following:

1. 1. The lack of unity in our churches and fellowships. There is conflict to some degree in most all churches. Spiritual unity is not the work of man but of the Spirit. We are to " Endeavor to keep the unity of the Spirit in the bond of peace." (Eph. 4:3.) The Spirit produces the unity in the believers, and the saints are to preserve the unity by being totally obedient to the scriptures.

2. 2.Another evidence that we need to be filled with the Spirit is the lack of the "fruit of the Spirit" in our lives. "The fruit (singular) of the Spirit is love, joy, peace, longsuffering, goodness, gentleness, meekness, faith, and temperance" or self-control. This is NOT the fruit of a Christian. It IS the fruit of the Spirit in a filled believer. Note that there are 9 facets of this fruit. Most all believers seem to have one or more of these naturally, and seem to think that if they keep working hard they will obtain the rest. The one or more that some believers seem to have is the result of the personality with which they were born and their disposition. But when one is filled with the Spirit, the Spirit produces all nine facets in their life. It is absolutely no problem for the Spirit to produce patience in an impatient man, or peace in an anxious man when they are under His control.

Has the Spirit produced love in your heart? Do you love God? Do you love your neighbor? If we are filled with the Spirit, then the love of God is shed abroad in our hearts by the Spirit. That means we love the sinners, the unlovely, our enemies, the homeless, and the people who take away our retirement fund as well as the man that gets rich at others loss. Of course we don't love their ways. We must love them.

Spirit-filled people are always praising God and the Lord Jesus Christ instead of complaining about everything that does not suit them. They give thanks continually, believing that their life is in the hand of God. Spirit-filled people always give generously. In Acts 2 and 4, the believers shared any and all of their possessions if and where needed. The Spirit-filled people were magnifying their leaders instead of being critical.

3. Another evidence of our need is the lack of witness and power in our churches.

   In one of America's largest and most evangelistic denominations, it takes 40 members one year to add one more person to their number. This includes the children of the members. Does this resemble the members of the early church where people were being saved daily, and sometimes by the hundreds and thousands? Some believers go their whole life and never lead one soul to Christ. And they are considered a normal believer, when in fact, it is abnormal.

4. There is also a great lack of Bible knowledge. It is appalling to read the results of some of the surveys taken about Bible knowledge and facts. How many church members do you know that know the scriptures to help someone be saved? Suppose that every member in your church were to lead one soul to Christ each year. What would be the result?

5. And then there is the lack of victorious living. Most believers seem to have accepted the defeated life as the normal planned and purposed by God. Most of the time it is difficult to tell a believer from a nonbeliever by his or her life. Jesus won the victory over Satan and the world. We need to believe that and let His Spirit produce that victory in us. God never planned for His people to be defeated by Satan at his will. He meant for us to be victorious over Satan, self, and sin. Then why are so many still living defeated lives?

In one of my pastorates, a deacon came to me one day all excited. He told me that he had just discovered that the man he had been working with for two years was a believer. While I was in agreement with him that it was wonderful that he had found out that his coworker was a believer, I couldn't help but wonder why he hadn't found out in the first few days of working with him. And since a Spirit-filled believer is obvious to another believer, my deacon's need for filling was very clear. I am glad to report that he soon was and became a powerful witness for Christ.

Have you ever been filled with the Holy Spirit? Are you seeing the fruit of the Spirit in your life? Is there a wonderful understanding of the scriptures as you read them? (1 Cor. 2:9-13.) Are answered prayers a normal thing in your life? Do you find it hard to believe all of the Bible as the Word of God? Are you having conflict with someone in your life? Are you generous in your support of the kingdom of God? Do you gladly and freely share with a brother of sister in need? Are you witnessing to and winning souls to Christ? Are you holding a grudge and un-forgiveness against someone? The right answers to the above questions will easily reveal if you are filled with the Spirit. If you are not, it seems from scripture that you need to be. Seek Jesus and His filling today.

Since you are a believer, why not be filled with the Holy Spirit? Happy filling!!!!

Chapter 5

Hindrances to the Spirit-Filled Life

Isa. 59:1-12; Acts 19:1-6

What hinders me from being filled with the Spirit of the living God? Am I not filled with the Spirit as I work and do my best? Doesn't God know the desire of my heart? Won't God fill me because He wants me to serve Him? Do I need to know all about the Spirit to be filled and walk in the Spirit? Why am I not filled now?

Have you ever wondered why more believers were not filled with the Spirit? Do you ever ask yourself the question, "Why doesn't the contemporary church look like the early church of the New Testament?" What does hinder us from measuring up to the early believers? God is the same as He was then. Is not man basically the same in his character and spirit?

There are many hindering causes that keep people from being filled with the Spirit. Perhaps only God knows them all. But there are four causes given plainly in scripture that do hinder us. One is:

IGNORANCE OF SCRIPTURE TEACHINGS

I have marveled at the number of people who are surprised by the teachings of scripture on the work of the Holy Spirit. Very few believers have a good working knowledge of the Bible. Many don't even know the simple plan of salvation, or why they are saved.

An example of ignorance of the Holy Spirit is in Acts 19:1-6. When Paul went to Ephesus, he found certain disciples, and it seemed evident to Paul that they had not been filled with the Holy Spirit. So he asked them, "Have you received the Holy Ghost since you believed?" (Acts 19:2)

Paul was very honest as well as bold. If you and I suspected that a brother had not been filled, would we have the boldness to ask him? Or would we say that it was none of our business? But because Paul was bold enough to ask in all honesty and meekness, the disciples were greatly profited.

The answer of the 12 disciples was, "We have not so much as heard whether there be any Holy Ghost." (Acts 19:2) Ignorance was their problem. Now their ignorance may have been justified in part because they did not have the scriptures as we do today. But ignorance was still their hindering cause. It is ours also. So many of us do not know at all, or we have a very fuzzy understanding of the work of the Holy Spirit. We are different from the disciples at Ephesus in that we have the scriptures. We just don't study them or don't believe them.

Sometimes our ignorance is the result of a pre-conceived idea of what the work of the Spirit is. Our "knowledge" or false knowledge comes from what we have heard others say rather than a study of the scriptures. Because we are acting on false knowledge, we miss the truth about the Holy Spirit's work in the life of a believer.

Then again, our ignorance of His work may come from a bias. Long before I was saved, I had heard so many negative things about people who were "baptized with the Holy Ghost", that when I became a believer, I shunned the idea. In spite of this I was filled with the Holy Spirit the first time only five months after I was saved. But I knew nothing about what had happened to me from scripture.

It was later that I was reading a book by Dr. R.A. Torrey on, The Holy Spirit, Who He Is, And What He Does, that I learned the truth from scripture. As I read his book about the filling of the Holy Spirit, it identified exactly what had happened to me. After searching the scriptures for weeks and months, I became thoroughly convinced that being filled by the Holy Spirit was an event in addition to and subsequent to being saved.

But ignorance of the Holy Spirit's work comes basically from a lack of study of the Word of God or a lack of faith.

A second hindrance to the Spirit-filled life is:

INDIFFERENCE TO THE HOLY SPIRIT'S FILLING

I think that indifference coupled with ignorance is one of the greatest causes of believers missing the blessings, benefits, and power of God in their life. I am not sure whether the indifference is the result of the ignorance, or the ignorance the result of the indifference. It may be both.

In the many Bible conferences and revivals I have been privileged to lead, most start at the Sunday morning service and continue either through Wednesday or Friday nights. The fact that manifests the indifference is the large number of people who are there on Sunday morning and indicate their indifference by never showing up for the rest of the week. They learn on Sunday morning about the benefits and blessings of the Spirit-filled life, but don't return to learn how to receive them. It seems to me that they either ignore it, discount it as worthy of their time, or just put it off to a more convenient time. Either way, they miss out and continue living in their carnal, or defeated, discouraged, depressed, and disappointed lives.

Yet a third hindrance to the Spirit-filled life is:

INFIDELITY OR UNBELIEF THAT EVERY BELIEVER MAY BE FILLED

There are some believers who think that the filling of the Holy Spirit is only for pastors, evangelists, missionaries and so on. They either feel that they are unworthy, or that because they are not in full time service to the Lord, they don't need His power. There are others that simply do not believe that one can be filled with the Holy Spirit at any given or subsequent time. Of course, the ideal is to walk in the Spirit, which has the idea of "remaining" full. But the truth is that we do not and often need to be filled again.

A good example of unbelief hindering God's people from receiving all that God had for them is the children of Israel in the wilderness when Moses led them out of Egypt to bring them to Canaan. It was the purpose of God to bring the children of Israel out of Egypt by Mt. Sinai and into the Canaan. Deut.6:23. It was not the purpose of God that they have to wonder 40 years in the wilderness.

Let me share that through many years of Bible study, I have learned that the promised land is not a type of heaven. I say this for several reasons. 1.) In heaven, there is no defeat, but there was at Ai. 2.) In heaven, there is no sin, but there was with Achan. 3.) In heaven there is no partial victory, but there was in the Canaan as the Israelites failed to drive out all of the inhabitants of the land. 4.) In heaven there is no death, but Joshua died as well as all the others.

Canaan is a type of the Spirit-filled life. It was the place for which God brought them out of Egypt to bring them in. It is the place where they were to possess their promised possessions. It was there that they were to realize God's power. It was there that they were to reach their own potential and fulfill God's purpose in their life.

All the Israelites who were twenty years old and older, who through unbelief, refused to follow Moses into Canaan, wandered and died in the wilderness in defeat, discouragement, despair, and disappointment. They could not go back across the Red Sea into Egypt, even though that is what they wanted to do. For the crossing of the Red Sea was their redemption from bondage and slavery.

God would not let them return to Egypt, which would be like us returning to our sin and bondage. They refused to go into Canaan because they did not believe that God was able to overcome their enemies. There was nothing left for them but 40 years of aimless wandering in the wilderness. They are a perfect example and type of the unbelieving Christian today who are wandering in their own spiritual wilderness.

In Hebrews chapters 3 and 4, God tells us that the Israelites did not enter into His rest---Canaan--- where they would be free from bondage, slavery, and cruel taskmasters--- because of their unbelief. Then God warns us that we will fail to enter into God's rest through our unbelief.

Then how can one have faith to be filled or to enter his promised land of milk and honey? I know only one way. That is to study the Bible concerning the Spirit-filled life. Believe what it says. There must be an interest and a thirst, thirst enough to drive us to the Bible to find His way to believe and to act on our faith. (John 7:37)

Another hindering cause to being Spirit-filled is

INIQUITY IN THE LIFE OF THE BELIEVER

Sin destroys. Sin destroys utterly. Sin destroys families, husbands, wives, children, communities, cities, and countries. Sin destroys our fellowship with God. Sin grieves the Holy Spirit in us. Sin quenches the Spirit. Sin destroys our confidence in God. Sin dulls our boldness to come to the throne of grace. Sin dampens our faith in God and ourselves. Sin in the life of a believer is one of the greatest causes of not being filled with the Holy Spirit even if we are seeking to be. This is not to say that if you live righteously and generally without sin, that you will be automatically filled. There are some other conditions to meet. It is to say that you cannot be filled with the Spirit if you are full of sin.

In Isaiah we read, "Behold, the Lord's hand is not shortened, that it cannot save; neither is his ear heavy, that it cannot hear: but your iniquities have separated between you and your God, and your sins have hid his face from you, that he will not hear." 59:1-2

Isaiah then goes on in the same passage to enumerate the sins of his society, which sounds very much like our society today.

In Jeremiah we read, "Your iniquities have turned away these things, and your sins have withheld good things from you." (5:25.) And "for mine eyes are upon all their ways: they are not hidden from my face, neither is their iniquity hid from mine eyes." (Jeremiah 16:17)

In Hebrews 4:13 we read, "Neither is there any creature that is not manifest in his sight, but all things are naked and opened to the eyes of him with whom we have to do."

God hears and sees and knows. Night and day are alike unto Him. We cannot hide our sin.

When you have prayed for a wayward or lost husband, or a wayward or lost son or daughter, and it seems like the heavens are brass, what is the problem? When a husband has prayed for a lost wife or son or daughter, and there is no answer, why not? When you have witnessed to a friend or neighbor and nothing but negative results, why doesn't God move in his life and save them? Why don't I have any power with God?

Isaiah says that it is not the Lord's problem, but our problem. God has not lost any of His ability to reach any person anywhere for anything. He will not hear our prayer nor answer it. He can reach out to save the one we have witnessed to and prayed for. It is our sin that prevents Him from acting on our behalf and saving that loved one.

This is in no way an effort just to make us feel guilty. It is an effort to help us to see ourselves as God sees us. It is an effort to keep us from being satisfied with ourselves, and letting the lost world go to hell. For as long as we have known sin, and unconfessed sin in our lives, we will not and cannot have the power of God in our life. Without the power of God in our lives we cannot win others to Christ nor influence them for good. We may not see our sin but they do. And because they do not see the presence and power of God in our life they think that we are no different than they.

I think that all of us know in our deepest being that we sin. Many of us have not confessed it and received forgiveness. Probably the three hardest words in the English language to say honestly and correctly are, "I have sinned" or "I am wrong." Pride often keeps us living with unconfessed sin. You may say, "My sins are so small and insignificant." But in God's sight, sin is sin, and is exceedingly sinful. "If we say that we have fellowship with God and walk in darkness, we lie and do not the truth. 1John 1:6

Then how can we be clean from our sin?

CONFESSION OF SIN

How then do I get rid of my sin and become acceptable to God? How can I have the power of God to witness with desired results, at least sometimes?

The answer to those two questions is found in 1 John 1:4-10 "And these things we write unto you, that your joy may be full. This then is the message that we have heard of him, and declare unto you, that God is light, and in him is no darkness at all. If we say that we have fellowship with him, and walk in darkness, we lie, and do not the truth: But if we walk in the light as he is in the light, we have fellowship one with another and the blood of Jesus Christ his Son cleanseth us from all sin. If we say that we have no sin, we deceive ourselves, and the truth is not in us. If we confess our sins, he is faithful and just to forgive our sins, and to cleanse us from all unrighteousness. If we say that we have not sinned, we make him a liar, and his word is not in us."

This portion of scripture says several things we need to heed:

1. The purpose of God in giving us this word is that our joy may be full!!

    God is light, sinless, and in Him
    is no darkness,(sin), at all.

    If we claim fellowship (not relationship) with Him
    and walk (live with) in darkness, (sin), we lie.

2. If we walk in the light like God does (without sin) we have fellowship with Him.

    If we have no unconfessed sin,
    the blood of Jesus Christ has cleansed us.

    If we deny that we are guilty of any unconfessed sin,
    we are deceiving OURSELVES,
    not others nor God.

3. If we confess our sins, He stands faithful and ready and just to forgive us and cleanse us.
4. To deny that there has been no sin in our life is to make God a liar and that we are not living by His word.

Confessing our sins from a repentant heart removes the trash from our lives and lets the grace of God flow in our lives.

While in school, I worked at the Rockwood Inn to help pay my way. It was my job to cook breakfast for about 45 people. After that I just did "handy work". One day the clean up crew in the kitchen ran out of water. They called on me for help.

The first thing I did was go up on the mountain behind the Inn to the huge cistern that caught the water coming through the pipeline from a large spring higher on the mountain. There was no water in the cistern, so I knew that the trouble was above the cistern.

I next went up to the spring on the mountain. There was water in abundance, thousands of gallons. I checked the strainer over the end of the pipe that carried the water from the spring to the cistern. That was fine. So I began to check the pipe at each joint to see if the water was flowing there.

After several joints of pipe I found where the water was not running. Somehow some trash had gotten through the strainer and clogged the line preventing the life-giving water from flowing to the reservoir. Did I put in a new pipeline? Did I find another spring? Did I replace the reservoir? I did none of these. I simply cleaned the trash out of the line and life-giving water began flowing again.

It is like that in the Christian life. We don't need a new Savior, or a new channel of grace, or to get saved again. We simply need to get the trash out of our lives. This we do by repenting and confessing our sins.

So we must confess our sins if we are to have the fullness of the Spirit. Confession is to say the same thing about our actions as God does. But there is a word about our confession.

1. We need to confess all of our sins to God. Not just that " we have sinned", or "if we have sinned", but that "I lied to Mary or John". "I stole money, or I lusted after Jim's new car or wife". Each individual act of sin must be confessed as the Spirit brings them into your mind. Don't try to think up sins. Just be still before God and with an open mind, waiting for Him to remind you.

2. Then we need to confess our sin to any one that we have sinned against.

3. Our confession must be as public as our sin. If no one but God knows about our sin, then our confession is to Him only. If no one else knows about our sin but God and the one we sinned against, then our confession is to them only. It is not necessary to confess publicly. But if we sinned publicly, then we need to confess publicly.

   As an example, suppose a pastor said something from the pulpit to or about an individual which was bad and he knew immediately that he was wrong. He should apologize right then. But instead, he waits until the service is over and goes to that person and apologizes. The person forgives him. But what about the rest of the congregation who were also offended by his remark? Not knowing that he had apologized to the person, and been forgiven, from then on when he speaks, all that they can "hear" is his offense to that person. It is the same way with us. We may confess to God and be forgiven by Him, but if we don't apologize to all who know our sin, it becomes a stumbling block to others and a hindrance to our filling.

4. When you have confessed your sin, accept and affirm forgiveness to yourself.

5. Forgive yourself. Sometimes this is the hardest to do. It will hinder you if you don't and Satan will bring it up to you repeatedly. It is our old nature that sins. It always will be. It will never be subject to God's word. It cannot be sanctified. (Rom. 8:7). Don't carry around a load of guilt unnecessarily. Have you confessed the same sin over and over again without having committed it again? Yet you still feel guilty. That is Satan trying to make you believe that God has not forgiven you. Forgive yourself.

When we have so confessed our sin, we can rejoice in the Lord and in the fact that we are cleansed. We know that our fellowship with God has been restored, and we are now prepared to be filled with the Spirit.

In one of my pastorates in New York, the wife of a couple with four or five children, ran off with another man and left the children with their dad. Not surprisingly, he was not a good housekeeper, but he was deeply hurt and he loved his children dearly. Of course, he had to continue to work to support the family, and was slack in some other things. Someone reported him to the Social Services Department in the county. The end result was that they took his children away from him and put them in foster homes in spite all that we could do. He made several efforts to get his children back, including getting his mother to move in with him to help with the house work and the children. All was to no avail.

A couple of months later, my friend made an appointment with the Director of the Social Services Department to try again to persuade her to let him have his children back. He asked me to go with him. I did. But nothing we could say or promise to do changed her in our favor. Finally in exasperation and anger, I told her what I thought of her in terms that were certainly wrong. But I thought that I had done my friend and the county a good service in letting her know our evaluation of her.

Sometime later I was scheduled to go to North Carolina to preach revivals on the Spirit- filled life in two different churches in successive weeks. My custom at the time was to begin my day at 5:00 AM with two hours of devotion and Bible study. On a Monday morning before

I was to leave to drive to North Carolina on Friday I asked God at the beginning of my devotion to reveal any sin in my life that would hinder my fellowship and power with Him. Immediately, and for the first time, He reminded me of what I had said to the Social Services Director and that I was to go and apologize.

I agreed to, but I didn't go. He reminded me of the same thing on each succeeding morning, and I promised each morning to go, but always found an excuse not to. I dreaded it worse than going to the dentist or a whipping. On Thursday morning before I was to leave on Friday at 4:00 AM, He reminded me that if I did not go to her and apologize, I need not go to North Carolina. There would be no revivals. It was a waste of my time and theirs. I went to see her. It was the hardest thing I ever did. I hoped that she wouldn't remember me. But when I appeared at her office door, she called me by my name and invited me in.

Just as quickly as I could, I told her that recently I had been seeking deeper fellowship with God, and He had reminded me of what I had said to her and demanded that I apologize to her. I did and asked her forgiveness. Her mouth dropped open in surprise and she forgave me. I left as quickly as I could, but oh, did I ever feel free and happy. I was overjoyed. I went to North Carolina and we had two tremendous revivals. One of the pastors told me that he had been pastoring 35 years, and it was the best revival he had ever experienced.

Confession of sin is hard, but has untold benefits with God. And I give this word of advice. If you need to confess a sin, the quicker you do it the easier it is to do. If you must eat crow, eat it while it is hot.

On the following pages is a tool that may help you become conscious of acts of sin in your life and something of the nature of sin. To use it let me suggest that you get alone and leisurely go over the list. On a separate sheet of paper mark those that you feel a twinge of conscience about by their number. At the end of the list, sit still before God and ask Him to continue to show you any other sin. Write them down on the separate sheet of paper and check them off as you confess them. There are some instructions at the end of the list that may help. If you do this, you will be absolutely cleansed by the blood of Jesus and ready to be filled with the Holy Spirit.

Since you are a believer, why not be filled with the Holy Spirit? !!! Happy filling!!!!

THE NAME OF THE GAME IS THE SELF LIFE.

God requires that we take a spiritual check on the self-life or ego on the throne of life.

A. 2 Cor. 13:5 "Examine yourselves whether you are in the faith; prove your own selves. Know you not your own selves that Jesus Christ is in you, except you are a reprobate."

B. 1 Cor. 11:28 "But let a man examine himself, and so let him eat of that bread and drink of that cup."

C. Rom. 14:12 "So then, every one of us shall given an account of himself to God."

D. Lamentations 3:40 "Let us search and try our ways, and turn again to the Lord."

The following are some of the evidences and manifestations of ego being on the throne of your life. God's Spirit alone can show and manifest this to your individual life. As you examine yourself according to the Word of God, are you conscious of:

1. A lofty feeling in view of your success in your business, ministry, or social position.
2. Self pride because of your family background or good looks.
3. Self pride because of your natural talents and accomplishments.
4. A feeling of importance when with others.
5. Being arrogant when with others.
6. The love of being noticed and the desire to be complimented.
7. An overflowing pride when noticed by contemporaries.
8. A love of being the leader in all spiritual and social activities.
9. References to yourself in all of your conversations.
10. An unholy pride of self when you have had liberty in speaking or praying in public.
11. Becoming angry or impatient with others; you call it nervousness or holy indignation.
12. A super sensitive spirit. (Easily offended)
13. Being resentful when contradicted by or reproved by others, even if they are right.
14. A desire to answer sharply those who are in authority over you.

15. An unwilling and an un-teachable spirit.
16. An argumentative spirit.
17. Reacting with a nasty, sarcastic, and vindictive spirit. Being vindictive.
18. Being so headstrong that you are not willing to see your sin as it really is.
19. A restless, overbearing spirit.
20. Being quick to criticize and find fault when not certain of conversation or activity.
21. Being fretful when forced to wait.
22. Being a person who loves to be persuaded and humored.
23. A spirit of fear of what man can do.
24. Running from duty when needed.
25. Justifying your failures.
26. Shrinking from duty because you have wealth or position.
27. A fearfulness that someone will not be in the spirit and will to agree with some person of statue.
28. Finding it easier to compromise rather than to take a stand.
29. Not wanting to admit the accomplishments or success of another.
30. A secret spirit of being envious of others.
31. Being willing to talk about the faults and failures of others rather than their successes.
32. Secret lust for someone of the opposite sex.
33. Unholy conversations and conduct with someone of the opposite sex.
34. Undue familiarity toward those of the opposite sex.
35. Wandering, un-baptized eyes. Lustful glances at the opposite sex.
36. Being dishonest and deceitful in small things.
37. Keeping the wrong friends and going to the wrong places.
38. The covering over of the truth.
39. Covering over and justifying your personal sins.
40. Making a better impression of yourself than is really true.
41. Failing to assume the responsibility of your call.
42. Being discouraged in time of stress and opposition.
43. Exaggeration in describing a truth.
44. False humility.

45. Straining the truth when counting the results.
46. Not trusting and having confidence in God and His power to perform.
47. Lack of faith in other Christians.
48. A guilty phobia of worrying and complaining in the midst of pain, or poverty, or other trials allowed by God.
49. Being overly anxious about whether thing will come out all right.
50. No concern for lost souls.
51. Indifference to the needs of the world.
52. No power with God.
53. Love of ease.
54. Procrastination.
55. Unholy love of material things.
56. Practicing hypocrisy.
57. Not praying for those who despitefully use you.
58. Covetousness of another's place of ministry.
59. Being too busy to hear a person in need of counseling and comforting.
60. Personal habits which are a hindrance to your testimony to the weak and unsaved.
61. Using slang and projecting foolish talk and jesting.
62. Talking or listening to unholy jokes and conversation.
63. Tale bearing and backbiting.
64. Not being courteous, forgiving, and kind.
65. Taking God's Name in vain.
66. Begin here to list your own private sins.

Note: Do not try to think up sins you have committed. Just relax and ask the Holy Spirit to bring to your remembrance what He wants you to confess and repent of. When you cease to hear His voice anymore, confess these sins one by one. Then write across the list, "The blood of Jesus Christ His Son cleanses me from all sin." Then destroy it!! Accept God's forgiveness and FORGIVE YOURSELF!!! Now you are ready for filling.

Chapter 6

Simple Steps to Being Filled with the Spirit

"Be not drunk with wine, wherein is excess, but be filled with the Spirit, speaking to yourselves in psalms, and hymns, and spiritual songs; singing and making melody in your heart to the Lord; giving thanks always for all things unto God and the Father in the name of our Lord Jesus Christ, submitting yourselves one to another in the fear of God." (Eph.5:18-21)

These are some of the most exciting verses in the New Testament. What an experience to worship God with the joy of the Lord in your heart as you sing praises to Him. In fact, when the first part of this verse is true, being filled with the Spirit, there is such an overwhelming joy that we can give thanks to God for everything and mean it, even the rough things that come in life, knowing that He is in control. So, if you are a believer, why not be filled with the Spirit?

There is a similarity in some who are drunk and one who is filled with the Spirit. On the day of Pentecost, the 12 were accused of being drunk. But Peter said, not so, "This is that which was spoken by the prophet Joel. In the last days saith God, I will pour out my Spirit upon all flesh." (Joel 2:28.)

In Ephesians, Paul also says in effect, if you want to be happy and uninhibited, don't get drunk with wine, but be filled with the Spirit. A drunk man is bold, uninhibited, and unashamed of what he is saying or doing. I believe these are the similarities in which a Spirit-filled person may be like the drunk man.

In teaching about the Spirit filled life, a friend of mine said, "A man gets drunk by drinking. Right? He gets more drunk by drinking more. Right? If these two examples mean anything, then one becomes filled with the Spirit by DRINKING, ..SPIRITUALLY!! To become filled more continuously with the Holy Spirit, he drinks more continuously... SPIRITUALLY."

"Jesus gave us three simple ways to be filled with the Holy Spirit. John 6:53 EAT HIS WORD!!! John 7:37. DRINK HIS WORD!!! John 20:22. BREATHE HIS WORD.

Jesus also taught us three simple requirements for filling... HUNGERING + THIRSTING + DRINKING = FILLING."

A man may be hungry, but if he will not eat, he is still hungry, right? A man may be thirsty, but if he will not drink, he is still thirsty, right? A man may stand in a grocery store full of food, and starve to death if he will not eat. A man may stand under a water- fall of life-giving water and die of thirst if he will not drink.

ARE YOU SPIRITUALLY HUNGRY TODAY? ARE YOU SPIRITUALLY THIRSTY TODAY? ARE YOU READY TO EAT AND DRINK NOW?

If you know that you have been born again, but you also know that you are not being filled with the Spirit then let me suggest that you do the following:

ACCEPT THE INDWELLING PRESENCE OF THE HOLY SPIRIT IN YOU RIGHT NOW

The Bible says in Eph. 1:13-14, " that we are sealed with the Holy Spirit of promise which is the earnest of our inheritance until the redemption of the purchased possession."

The indwelling Spirit is our guarantee of ultimate and final redemption, spirit, soul, and body. God, dwelling in us in the person of the Holy Spirit, says to us, "I will never leave you nor forsake you" (Heb. 13:5.)

Affirm this fact in and to yourself, that you are indwelt by the Holy Spirit all the time. Say to yourself, "The Holy Spirit lives in me." Say it until you are persuaded by it if you are having trouble believing it.

This is not just psyching yourself up, it is confessing the word of God until the power of God is released in your life to believe. Affirm it as often as you need to.

Trust God's Word Above And Over Everything Else.

Look at these examples of His indwelling presence for confirmation:

The Holy Spirit will abide with you forever. John 14:16
God has given the Holy Spirit unto those who obey Him. Acts 5:32
The Holy Spirit which is given unto us. Rom. 5:5
He, the Spirit, shall be in you. John 14:17
The Holy Spirit, Whom God has shed on us abundantly. Titus 3:5
God has given unto us His Holy Spirit. 1 Thess. 4:8
Having begun in the Spirit. Gal. 3:3
The Holy Spirit which is in you. 1 Cor. 6:19
The Spirit of God dwelleth in you. 1 Cor. 3:16
The Holy Spirit dwells in you. Rom. 8:9, 11

Obviously, God wants us to know that He lives in us. We are the temple of the Holy Spirit. We are the habitation of God through the Spirit. Far too many believers relegate Him to the foyer or the closet of our life. He does not have the free run and reign in our life. We are not making Him Lord continuously but He is there, all the time. A strong conviction of this truth is essential to being filled with the Holy Spirit.

I was leading a seminar on the Spirit-filled life in New York State. This certain woman had attended every night until the last night in which my subject was How To Be Filled. She had to miss for reasons beyond her control. She was so thirsty for filling she requested that I go over the subject with her the next day. I did, and she was wonderfully filled. After rejoicing for a good while, she sat very quietly for a spell with tears just streaming down her cheeks. I asked if she was having a problem. Her answer amazed me as to her grasp of the truth. She said, "No, no problem. I was just sitting here in my mind's eye watching Jesus go through my closets and chest of drawers. This lady had already turned it all over to Jesus including her wardrobe.

A Thirst For Jesus' Filling.

Jesus said in John 7:37-39, "If any man thirst, let him come unto me, and drink. He that believeth on me, as the scriptures have said, out of his belly shall flow rivers of living water. But this spake he of the Spirit, which they that believe on him should receive….."

Thirst for God and His fullness is one of the most critical requirements for being filled. God does not give His fullness to the careless and uncaring. He will not fill one who is satisfied with a mediocre life. When there is an intense thirst for God, one is usually willing and ready to meet the other requirements. But only as one is thirsting for God enough to lay aside other things that he may hold dear, things that are a hindrance to being filled, is he ready for God to fill with His Holy Spirit.

David expressed this kind of thirst when he wrote, "As the hart panteth after the water brooks, so panteth my soul after thee, O God. My soul thirsteth for God, for the living God…." (Psa. 42:1-2.) In Psa. 63:1-2. David said, "O God, thou art my God; early will I seek thee: my soul thirsteth for thee; my flesh longeth for thee in a dry and thirsty land where no water is; to see thy power and thy glory, so as I have seen thee in the sanctuary."

Too many Christians have other things that are more important to them. Those things may be hindering their being filled with the Spirit. Yet, they are not thirsty enough for the living God to fill them.

I once saw an old western movie. The cowboy had started out across the desert with his horse, saddle, canteen, six-guns and rifle. All of these were very important to him. He would not easily have parted with any of them. But it was farther than he thought across the desert. He used all the water in his canteen for himself and his horse. They plodded on. But the horse didn't last long without water and the cowboy had to put him down.

He picked up his saddle, which was his favorite, threw it over his shoulder, took his rifle, which he thought he couldn't do without, and started out toward the other side of the desert. But it wasn't long before the heavy saddle became a hindering burden. As badly as he hated to leave it, he wanted to reach the other side more, so it threw it away.

He plodded on and soon threw his empty canteen away. The farther he went, the more the rifle and six-guns slowed him down and took extra energy to carry. He finally threw them away. He was willing to put anything and everything aside that hindered him from reaching the other side. We need to come to the place that we thirst for the living God like that. When we do we will gladly leave anything behind in order to drink from the fountain of living water. Then we are close to the condition for God to entrust His power to us and fill us.

The absence of such thirst in a believer's life is caused by the presence of sin, or the failure to drink His promises. If the absence of thirst in your life is caused by your failure to drink His promises, by all means open your Bible and start drinking and keep on drinking. What Jesus really said in John 7:37-39 was that if we would drink and keep **on** drinking, then there would flow and keep on flowing rivers of living water from our lives. Notice that he did not say a stream, or a trickle, or a drip, or not even a river, but rivers, plural.

Have you been around a believer that just seemed to unconsciously overflow on you? Have you ever wondered why that believer had so much joy and enthusiasm for the things of God? It is because he was drinking on a regular basis. Now drinking is simply the process by which we get something we want that is outside of us inside of us. In the case of thirst for the truths of God, we drink by reading, studying and believing and doing the word of God.

Confess Our Sins

If the cause of the absence of thirst in your life is caused by sin, then we not only need to do the above, but we need to confess our sins. This means that we are to confess and repent of each sin the Holy Spirit shows us, or that we know to be in our life. It is not enough to say "if I have sinned". We all have. We must confess our sins one by one and turn from them. When we do this we receive God's forgiveness. We need to sit quietly before the Lord, asking Him to show us any hindering causes, and as He does, write them down. Get them all up to date as nearly as you can. When He has finished showing us sins for today, we confess them and write across our paper 1 John 1:9. Then we are to forgive ourselves. This needs to be a daily process. We are now ready for the next step.

ASK GOD TO FILL YOU BY FAITH

Now ask God to fill you. Simply knowing you need to be or wishing you were filled is not adequate. Just like it is not adequate for one to know that he ought to be saved, or to wish he were. Asking or seeking is absolutely a part of salvation and being filled with the Spirit.

In Luke 11:11-13 Jesus said, "If a son shall ask bread of any of you that is a father, will he give him a stone? Or if he ask a fish, will he for a fish give him a serpent? Or if he ask an egg, will he for an egg give him a scorpion? If ye then, being evil, know how to give good gifts to your children: how much more shall your heavenly Father give the Holy Spirit to them that ask him?"

I am not the best father by any means. But I know this, that if one of my children or grandchildren came to me hungry and asked for something to eat, I would do everything in my power to give him good food. I certainly wouldn't mock him by giving something that would make him sick. God says, if we who are evil will gladly give our children food when they are hungry, how much MORE will our heavenly Father give us the Holy Spirit when we ask Him.

Like all of the rest of God's promises, we must ask in faith, believing. If we doubt that God will fill us with the Holy Spirit, then He won't. It is as simple as that. We must believe that God means what He says, and will respond to our request as quickly as He will to any one's. In fact, if everyone else in the world asked unbelieving, they would not receive, and at the same time you asked believing, you would receive.

In Galatians 3:13-14 we read, "Christ hath redeemed us from the curse of the law, being made a curse for us……..that the blessings of Abraham might come on the Gentiles through Jesus Christ: that we might receive the promise of the Spirit through faith."

So we must ask in faith. You say, but suppose it isn't God's will to fill me. Or how do I know it is God's will to fill me with His Spirit? In Eph. 5:18, we read, "Be not drunk with wine wherein is excess, but be filled with the Spirit." In this verse God commands us to be filled. God doesn't command us to do something that isn't His will. So we know that it is His will for us to be filled.

How do I know that God has filled me?

In 1 John 5:14-15, we read, "And this is the confidence that we have in him, that if we ask anything according to his will, he heareth us. And if we know that he hears us, whatsoever we ask, we know that we have the petition that we desired of him."

So, we know that it is His will to fill us with the Spirit, and we know that He hears us when we ask according to His will. We also know by faith that we are filled because we asked according to His will. Filling does not depend on feelings. So many miss the mark at this point. The sequence is first fact, then faith, then feelings. Sometimes the manifestation and feelings come later, but we need to believe and affirm now.

Once when I was leading a seminar at Ridgecrest Baptist Assembly on the Spirit-filled life, there were two ladies from North Carolina who were obviously thirsting to be filled. They asked God to fill them, but they didn't feel like He had. I told them that they must go by faith and not feeling. But they returned home without a confidence of being filled. The two ladies eventually persuaded their pastor to invite me to their church for a week on the same emphasis.

The first night when I gave the invitation these two ladies came forward wanting to be filled with the Spirit. They thought they never had been, so I encouraged them to ask by faith. They still looked disappointed. So I encouraged them to affirm to themselves that God had been faithful and answered their request. I said to them to say out loud, " I am filled with the Holy Spirit." I had them repeat it several times. After several times of affirming to themselves that they were filled, I saw a glow beginning to come in their faces. They confessed the word of God and it released the power of God in their life. I suggested that they go home that night and tell someone that they were filled with the Holy Spirit., They did. From that time on they never doubted.

Faith is an absolute essential to being filled with the Spirit as well as being saved. So ask Him to fill you. Right now!! Believe Him, that you are filled. Right now!! Affirm it to yourself right now!. Now thank Him for filling you!! You have just taken a drink by faith at the fountain of Jesus. Date your filling. This is just the first time for filling. There will be many more. We leak!! Every time we sin, we will need to confess that sin and go through the same steps again.

NOW ALLOW THE LORD TO WORK THROUGH YOU

It is important for us not to try to do a work, and ask God to bless that work. Now you will be letting God choose what and where your work will be, and allow Him to do it through you. There is a big difference. When we find out what God wants us to do, we need to get involved there. That is where God will really bless His work that you are doing.

Each Christian must learn just how God deals with them. He may not deal with each believer the same way. There are several ways that God reveals to me what He wants me to do. One is what the scriptures says for me to do. Another one is that He makes certain scriptures come alive to me. Another is when an opportunity comes to serve that is related to the scriptures that were quickened to me. Still another is that, especially if it is long range, God will begin to burden my heart and mind with whatever it is He wants done. If it comes today and is "gone tomorrow", I know that it is not of God. But if the burden persists, then I am fairly assured that it is His will for me to do it. You probably have your own way of determining how God works in your life.

As an example, in 1961, God began to burden my heart and mind about starting new churches in the cities and villages where there was little or no gospel witness. After 6 months of seeking, praying, and listening, I resigned my pastorate in South Carolina, and with fear and trembling, moved my family to New York State.

There was no church to go to, no job to go to, no house to live in, and only one mother and her three daughters to begin a work with. But God's burden had stayed with me and grew heavier in all those six months. I was a green-horn in mission work. I had only been pastoring six years. I was a novice. But we went and God provided our needs. Twenty two years later, God had started 28 churches with me and the other cohorts that He had sent to help. How I praise His name. Now that you are learning to be Spirit filled, let God work through you.

ABIDE IN CHRIST

The abiding in Christ life has no unconfessed sin in it. As soon as a person abiding in Christ sins, he immediately repents and confess that sin, ask to be filled again, and go on abiding.

The abiding life in Christ has no corner or closet in his life into which Christ is not invited to be Lord. No life in which He cannot share.

The abiding life is one that looks to Jesus for all wisdom needed for life. He looks to Jesus, the author and finisher of our faith, for the answers to all of life's problems and continually seeks God's plan for his life.

The abiding life makes Jesus Lord of EVERYTHING!!! Let Christ take over everything in your life. Your life will be completely turned around. This is the NORMAL Christian life.

Since you are a believer, why not be filled with the Holy Spirit?

Happy filling!

Chapter 7

Dealing With the Devil

Now that you have been filled with the Spirit, you will immediately encounter three enemies. They are self, sin and Satan. We deal with self by counting ourselves crucified with Christ. More about this later. We deal with sins by confessing and repenting of them. We dealt with that enemy in previous chapters. But how do we deal with the devil? We are no match for him. Not in our own strength. But in God's provision for dealing with him, it is as simple and as easy as dealing with the other two enemies!! We must deal with him effectively if we are to walk in the Spirit. He will continually seek to drag us down into defeat. He is sly and subtle. "Finally, my brethren, be strong in the Lord and the power of his might. Put on the whole armour of God that ye may be able to stand against the wiles of the devil. For we wrestle not against flesh and blood but against principalities, against powers, against the rulers of the darkness of this world, against spiritual wickedness in high places." (Eph. 6:10-12)

IDENTIFY YOUR ENEMY

The first step in any battle is to identify your enemy; otherwise we are just flailing the air. Now God says that our enemy or enemies are not flesh and blood. That immediately rules out any other person from being our enemy. It rules out our husband or wife. It rules out the pastor and the deacons. It rules out our neighbor, at home and at church. They are all flesh and blood, and are NOT our enemy. The enemy is not the charismatics, the liberals, or the fundamentalists. Our enemy is the devil and his angels.

Our enemies are the principalities and powers, and rulers of the darkness of this world.

God says again in 1 Peter 5:8, "Be sober, be vigilant: because your adversary the devil, as a roaring lion, walketh about seeking whom he may devour." So the devil and his helpers are our enemies, and they only. So they are who our battles are against.

If we are to win the battle with Satan, we must fight that battle with God's weapons instead of our own. In 2 Cor. 10:3-5, we are told that we are to make war against the enemy, not in the flesh, but in the Spirit. We are not to use our carnal weapons, but God's, which are mighty through God to the pulling down of any strongholds in our life, or sometimes in the lives of others. "⁴ (For the weapons of our warfare *are* not carnal, but mighty through God to the pulling down of strong holds;) ⁵ Casting down imaginations, and every high thing that exalteth itself against the knowledge of God, and bringing into captivity every thought to the obedience of Christ;" (2 Cor 10:4-5)

So what are these weapons and how do we use them?

DEALING WITH THE ENEMY

The first thing God tells us in Ephesians 6 is to be strong in the Lord. Now there is a big difference in being strong FOR the Lord, and in being strong IN the Lord. Being strong FOR the Lord happens when we try to fight the devil in our own strength for God's sake. God doesn't need us to do that. He can take care of His own battles. But being strong IN the Lord is when we use God's provided way and strength to defeat the devil. Jesus has already defeated the devil. He has won the victory. He did it by and through His death on the cross. (Heb. 2:14). "¹⁴ Forasmuch then as the children are partakers of flesh and blood, he also himself likewise took part of the same; that through death he might destroy him that had the power of death, that is, the devil;" (Heb 2:14)

He wants us to be strong in Him. To illustrate, let us go to the world of machinery. If I am being strong FOR a bulldozer, I am trying to help the bulldozer push over a tree with my puny strength. But I can be strong IN the bulldozer by handling the controls in accordance with the manufactures' instructions. By following their instructions, I can push over a tree simply by the moving of my fingers and hands.

The manufacturer has provided for the power to push over the tree, but only through following their instructions. That is the only way.

Likewise, when we follow our Manufacture's instructions, we are strong in Him, and can easily defeat the enemy. But it can be done no other way. We can try to substitute here and there but it just won't work.

THE WHOLE ARMOR OF GOD

Ephesians 6:10-17 gives us directions in how to dress ourselves with the armor of God. In putting on His whole armor, we will be able to stand against the wiles of the devil. What articles of spiritual clothing does the whole armor of God include?

We are told by the Manufacturer in 1 Peter 5: -11, that we are to be humble and submissive to others. We are to put away pride for God resists the proud and gives grace to the humble. We are to cast the care of battle on Him when we have properly dressed for battle. We are to be sober and vigilant. I see this instructing us to be serious and not frivolous. We are to be wide awake and alert to the devils wiles.

We are to resist the devil "in the faith", not just by faith. "In the faith" tells me that I am to wage my battle with the devil with all the tools that are given me by God in the body of scriptures that make up the faith. God tells me that I can withstand the attacks of the devil if I will follow the instructions He has given in His Word.

We are to have our loins girt about with truth. Lying and exaggeration give the devil a place, which we are instructed in Ephesians not to do. (Eph. 4:27). Every time we tell a lie, we set ourselves up for having to tell another one. In all our ways we are to be honest and above board. We can lie by telling a half truth, or a certain part of the truth to give the wrong impression.

In order to defeat the devil, we must have on the breastplate of righteousness. Probably this speaks of positional righteousness which we have through faith in Jesus, and practical righteousness which we have by obedience to God's Word.

We are to have our feet shod with the preparation of the gospel of peace. I hear our Lord telling us to be prepared, as we travel through life, to correctly apply the truths of the gospel to any situation the devil confronts us with. The preparation makes the difference. I like to eat.

My wife goes to the grocery store and buys several bags of groceries. She comes home and puts them on the table. To be honest, they do not look too appetizing in their raw state. But when she has taken time and knowledge to prepare them properly, they are very delicious and desirable. But the preparation takes knowledge, work, and time. In preparing the Word of God, the truth, we need to learn to know which scriptures apply to which situation. We need to know more than just one scripture. This takes a lot of study and work

The shield of faith is also absolutely necessary to win the battle. "Without faith, it is impossible to please God." (Heb. 11:6). The battle is the Lord's. We are simply to trust His instructions and do them. But to win the battles it is necessary to believe God's Word. We may not understand it, but we must believe it and act on it. He then gives us the victory. Faith in God's Word pours water on all of Satan's fiery darts.

I also am to wear the helmet of salvation into battle. In the military, when one goes into battle, he must wear a steel helmet. It helps to protect his head from bullets and shrapnel. One can be wounded in many places in his body and get over it, but the head is very vulnerable. We are equally vulnerable when we are not sure of our salvation. But when you are saved and sure, you can tell the devil he can't get around or through the blood of Jesus.

The sword of the Spirit, the Word of God, is our most powerful weapon. When Jesus was tempted by Satan, he used the Word of God as His weapon. Jesus told the devil exactly what God had said about each temptation. Now be careful at this point. Satan will quote or misquote the Word of God to you as he did to Jesus. He does this by applying the Word of God to the incorrect situation.

It is interesting how nearly every piece of armor is connected to the Word of God. The loin girth with truth. "Thy Word is truth." The breastplate of righteousness is attained from believing His written Word and receiving His Living Word. Obeying His Word gives us practical righteousness. The preparation of the gospel of peace is part of the written word.The shield of faith comes by hearing and reading and believing the Word.

The helmet of salvation comes from hearing of and believing in the Living Word, even Jesus. The sword of the Spirit is the Word of God. And prayer depends on God's Word to know what He promises and will answer.

A person who tries to defeat the devil without a fairly good knowledge of the Word of God is in trouble. That person will probably become the victim. Thank God for His infallible and inerrant Word. Use it as an effective weapon against the devil.

TAKE OUR STAND IN THE LORD

Four times in Ephesians 6:11-14, we are told to stand, in vs. 11, 2 times in 13, and 14.

This means we are to assume our position in Christ. 11 times in the first 13 verses of chapter one of Ephesians it is stated that we are "in Christ", or "in Him". So when we have identified the enemy, and have put on the whole armor of God, we are to take our stand in Christ against the enemy.

According to God's Word in Eph. 1:19-20, the power of God that raised Jesus from the dead and sat Him at His right hand is available to the believer. In 1 Peter 3:22, all angels, powers and principalities are subject to Christ. It naturally follows that if we are in Christ, they are also subject to us.

A word of caution must be observed here. Be absolutely sure that you are saved, in Christ, and that you have on the WHOLE armor of God. You must stand with the confidence that you are a child of God, covered by the blood of Jesus, and because you are in Christ you are greater than the devil. "Greater is he that is in you, than he that in the world." (1 John 4:4). The Holy Spirit lives in His children and He is greater than Satan. Believe it. So stand tight and withstand the devil's wiles and devises.

In taking your stand, assume your victory over the devil, IN CHRIST. Jesus won the victory over Satan on the cross. "Forasmuch then as the children of God are partakers of flesh and blood, he also himself likewise took part of the same, that through death he might destroy him that had the power of death, that is, the devil" Heb. 2:14. Satan's power to harm a believer has been destroyed if that believer will stand in Jesus Christ to do his battles.

The following scriptures should encourage God's children in their battle with Satan.

On the cross, Jesus "having spoiled principalities and powers, and made a show of them openly, triumphing over them in it." (Col. 2:15) "For this purpose was the Son of God manifested, that he might destroy the works of the devil." (1 John 3:8).

"Now thanks be unto God, which always causes us to triumph in Christ, and maketh manifest the savour of his knowledge by us in every place." (2 Cor. 2:14)

Child of God, assume the victory that Christ won for you on the cross. He won it. You just walk in it by faith. Stand fast as you face the devil knowing and affirming that the victory is yours because Christ won it.

In taking your stand assume your authority IN CHRIST. If Christ is seated at the right hand of God with authority over all principalities and powers, that includes the devil. We are in Christ. Do we not have the authority of Christ over Satan if we are in Him, abiding in Him, and in faith stand against him?

Our authority does not come from our self, but from Christ. All the authority of heaven is ours if you use it under Christ. Let me illustrate.

I can stop an eighteen wheeler running 60 miles an hour!! I can stop it with one hand!!

I can put on a state trooper's uniform, walk out in front of that truck, hold up one hand, and that truck driver will lock down the brakes if he has to in order to stop. Now what made him stop? Was it me, or the uniform that I was wearing? It was the uniform.

Now consider this. As a state trooper, I could be assigned to go to a certain spot and stop eighteen wheelers for one reason or another. I drive to that spot. I even turn on my flashing lights. But as long as I sit in that car or stand by the side of that road wondering or doubting the trucks will stop, they won't. They will keep whizzing by!! If I believe that I have all the authority of the state behind me, by faith I walk out in the road and hold up my hand. The trucker recognizes the uniform, knows that the authority and power of the whole state backs it up, and dares not refuse to stop. That is, if he knows what is good for him!!

Satan recognizes the armor of God. He knows that it has all the authority of heaven behind it! We are told to resist the devil. (James 4:7). We are to resist him dressed in God's armor. (Eph. 6:11-14). We are to resist him in the faith. (1 Peter 5:9). We are to resist him through the death and blood of Jesus Christ. (Heb. 2:14; 1 John 4:4). We are to resist him in Jesus Name! God promises that when we do this, he, the devil, will flee from us. (James 4:7).

Believer, can you believe the Word of God enough to "walk out in the road" ahead of Satan and hold up your hand in the Name of Jesus, believing you have all of heaven's authority behind you? If so, you have achieved another very important truth in helping you deal victoriously with the devil. When you have victoriously dealt with sin, self, and Satan, the three enemies of righteousness, you are now free to be filled with the Spirit and "walk in the Spirit, and not fulfill the lust of the flesh." (Gal. 5:16).

Since you are a believer, why not be filled with the Holy Spirit?!!!

Happy dealing!

Chapter 8

How to Walk in the Spirit

Gal. 5:16-23 reads: "This I say then, walk in the Spirit, and ye shall not fulfill the lust of the flesh. For the flesh lusteth against the Spirit, and the Spirit against the flesh: these are contrary the one to the other: so that ye cannot do the things that ye would. But if ye be led of the Spirit, ye are not under the law. Now the works of the flesh are manifest, which are these: Adultery, fornication, uncleanness, lasciviousness, idolatry, witchcraft, hatred, variance, emulations, wrath, strife, seditions, heresies, envyings, murders, drunkenness, revellings, and such like: Of which I tell you before, as I have also told you in time past, that they which do such things shall not inherit the kingdom of God. But the fruit of the Spirit is love, joy, peace, longsuffering, gentleness, goodness, faith, meekness temperance: against such there is no law."

Every born again believer now has two natures that battle for his obedience, the flesh and the Spirit. The flesh is the nature he was born with, and the Spirit is the nature he was born again with. Other names used in scriptures synonymous with the flesh are: the old man, the body of sin(Rom. 6:6), the law of sin, the body of this death, as used in Rom. 7:23-24, the carnal man (Rom 8:7). God has provided for the crucifixion of the old man, Rom. 6, which will be dealt with in a later chapter. This is necessary for us to walk in the Spirit.

One of the main ideas of walking in the Spirit is that we not fulfill the lust of the flesh. That is, not be controlled by our old nature. I believe that it is the desire of every child of God to walk in the Spirit. We get tired and frustrated with the continual battle that we have with the flesh. I know from personal experience that I have hated and been sickened by some of my actions as a child of God. With the apostle Paul I cry out, "Who shall deliver us from the body of this death?" (Rom. 7:24). Is not this the cry of every serious child of God? We hate the works of the flesh, and especially when we allow them in our life. The answer is to walk in the Spirit and we will no longer yield to our enemy, the old man.

HOW DO I WALK IN THE SPIRIT?

How then do I walk in the Spirit? One must first be filled with the Spirit before one can walk in the Spirit. Being filled with the Spirit is not a once and for all experience. There are many fillings as revealed in Acts 2:4; 4:8; 4:31; 5:32; 6:3, 8. Being filled with the Spirit does not exempt us from the war between the flesh and the Spirit. In fact, Satan may work on you even harder because you have been filled. But walking in the Spirit is kind of like being filled on a continual basis.

To walk in the Spirit we must do the following: Each of our individual sins that is un-confessed must be confessed. When we sin we interrupt the flow of the Spirit from our Lord Jesus Christ. But He stands ready to forgive and restart the flow of "rivers of living water" when we repent and confess our sins. His precious blood cleanses us from the sin and we simply ask Him to fill us again

When you have confessed your sin and asked God to fill you with His Spirit again, thank Him for filling you, and believe that He has. Remember, you are filled by faith, and not by feeling. Just go on in faith, knowing that God heard your prayer because it is the will of God to fill you if you are clean. You may not feel any or much different, but you are. Affirm to yourself that you are filled. You continue to walk in obedience to His Word and the confidence that He is with you and upon you in power. In Col. 2:6 we read, "As you have received Christ Jesus the Lord, so walk ye in him."

We received Him by faith. We are to walk by faith that we have been obedient to His Word and we are being filled. Entirely too many of God's children miss out precisely at this point. They demand to "feel" something. Some do, some don't. After you are continuing to walk in the Spirit, then you should feel something. You should feel the fruit of the Spirit that He is producing in your life, love, joy, peace, longsuffering, goodness, gentleness, faith, meekness, and self-control. It has been my experience, that when I am filled and walking in the Spirit, there is an overwhelming sense of love and joy and peace in serving Him.

KEEP SELF ON THE CROSS

Self, that is your old nature, is your worst hindrance to you walking in the Spirit. Self wants to "do what comes naturally." Romans 6:6 tells us that, "Knowing this, that our old man is crucified with him, that the body of sin might be destroyed, that henceforth we should not serve sin." Note particularly that the Word says "knowing this." You can count on it. You can take it to the bank. It is a sure thing. Your old man is crucified with Christ. He IS crucified, not shall be, or needs to be. He is.

Therefore, count or "reckon ye also yourselves to be dead indeed unto sin", and equally so, reckon yourself "alive unto God through Jesus Christ our Lord." (Rom. 6:11)

"I am crucified with Christ, nevertheless I live, yet not I, but Christ liveth in me. And the life that I now live, I live by the faith of the Son of God, who loved me and gave himself for me." (Gal. 2:20) "And they that are Christ's have crucified the flesh with the affections and lusts." (Gal. 5:24).

The flesh is self. So every time you are tempted to sin, count that you are crucified with Christ. Therefore you are dead to sin. A dead corpse cannot respond to any stimuli. You are dead to sin, but alive unto God. When you count it so and affirm it to yourself, it becomes a reality in your life.

This was my hardest battle for years of seeking to walk in the Spirit. My experience said to me that I am alive to sin. I sin every day. I respond to temptation by yielding. But the Word says that I am crucified, and therefore I am dead to temptation or sin. I had to ask myself, "Now who is right, you or the Word of God?" It took an awful lot of affirmation to myself of what the Word said before I could take it by faith, because it seemed so contrary to my experience. Then one day after reading Romans 6 about a dozen times, I said out loud to my-self and to God, "God, I am dead to sin, and I am alive unto you through Jesus Christ my Lord."

So I began practicing telling myself and Satan that. It worked. I began having a new freedom from the power of sin. But I also found out that it is something that I have to do each time I am tempted. It is not a once-and-for-all situation. Self will creep down off the cross and get back on the throne of your heart. It does it so slyly that you won't even realize what it is doing until you have yielded. But as you practice counting yourself dead to sin it becomes easier. After some time it will almost come automatically to do it.

It is kind of like driving a car with a stick shift. When you are first learning to drive one, you have to think of depressing the clutch, letting up on the gas, shifting the gears, releasing the clutch, and pressing on the gas. It takes a while to get it all together. But after you become an experienced driver, you go through the motion without even thinking of what you are doing. It will become that way with counting yourself dead to sin and alive unto God.

THE LAW OF CO-CRUCIFIXION

[2] For the law of the Spirit of life in Christ Jesus hath made me free from the law of sin and death. [3] For what the law could not do, in that it was weak through the flesh, God sending his own Son in the likeness of sinful flesh, and for sin, condemned sin in the flesh: [4] That the righteousness of the law might be fulfilled in us, who walk not after the flesh, but after the Spirit. (Romans 8:2-4)

Let me illustrate how this principal works. It is the law of sin that pulls you down. But the law of co-crucifixion—being crucified with Christ--is greater and is able to overcome or override the law of sin. May I use an illustration from aerodynamics. The law of gravity has such a pull on the plane that it sits on the ground. It cannot and does not rise until it begins to obey the law of aerodynamics. When the pilot and the plane obey the law of aerodynamics the plane rises and flies. It will continue to fly as long as the law of aerodynamics is obeyed. When a plane ceases to fly it is always because that law is not obeyed. The law of gravity is still in effect, but the law of aerodynamics is greater and supersedes the law of gravity.

Now that is a well established law. Millions of people believe it, and it works for them to fly from place to place. Now just suppose that you want to travel from where you live to a city thousands of miles away. You feel sure that you can go safely by train or ship, or car. But you don't have the time. You can fly quickly. But you just can't believe that the law of aerodynamics is greater or supersedes the law of gravity. You can read all about planes and their ability to fly. You can listen to the testimony of all your neighbors and friends of how they have flown. You can even buy a ticket to the destination. But until you go to the airport and get on that plane, you will not get to where you want to go. In flight you might even try to help the plane fly. Or you might be afraid. But as long as the pilot and the crew make that plane obey the law of aerodynamics, you will get there without your help, or in spite of your fears.

It is the same way with the law of co-crucifixion and the law of sin. As long as you practice the law of co-crucifixion, you will overcome the law of sin. But if you cease to practice that law, the law of sin quickly takes over, and down you go. Romans 8:2 says, "For the law of the Spirit of life in Christ Jesus has set me free from the law of sin and death."

Now that you are learning to practice the law of co-crucifixion you can rejoice in the Lord.

REJOICE IN THE LORD

The Bible tells us to "Rejoice in the Lord always, and again I say, rejoice." (Phil. 4:4).

But you may think that you don't have anything to rejoice over. You may be afflicted or under heavy trials or in prison. You may have just lost your fortune or one or more of any number of burdens. What do you have to rejoice about? Rejoice that you are in the Lord. Rejoice over your position and salvation in Him. Rejoice over whose you are, who you are, what you are, what He is, and who He is.

Rejoice always. In the good times and in the bad times. When it rains, and when it snows. When the sun shines and when it is cold. You don't have to rejoice in your circumstances, but in the Lord. Not only if the occasion justifies, but always. The joy of the Lord will be your strength. Complaining and grumbling over your circumstances just gives Satan an opportunity to make you doubt God's goodness and love for you. Rebuke the devil and he will flee from you.

Give thanks for and in all things. Now that takes faith in God for sure. But the Word tells us to give thanks in everything.

"In everything give thanks, for this the will of God in Christ Jesus concerning you." (1 Thess. 5:18). So you say that is just to give thanks in the midst of every situation. That is certainly true. But the Bible also tells us in Eph. 5:20 "Giving thanks always for all things unto God and the Father in the name of our Lord Jesus Christ."

This is said in the context of having just been filled with the Spirit. The Spirit-filled believer can give thanks for all things at all times because he knows that God loves him. He knows that he is called according to God's eternal purpose. He knows that God is at work in his life to make ALL things work together for his good. Yes it takes faith, but no more than a grain of mustard seed if the faith is in God.

So by the grace of God, Who made provisions for you to walk in the Spirit, so that you would not fulfill the lust of the flesh, so walk. So walk with faith, joy, and thanksgiving, to God the Father, and to the Lord Jesus Christ.

Since you are a believer, why not be filled with the Holy Spirit? Happy walking!!

Chapter 9

The Fruits of the Spirit

"For the fruit of the Spirit is in all goodness, and righteousness, and in truth." (Eph. 5:9)

Notice that in the chapter heading, I used the word "fruits", plural. I have previously said that the "Fruit" of the Spirit is singular. In Gal. 5:22-23, it is. In that passage there are nine facets of that fruit. It is the fruit of the Spirit that He produces in the life of a Spirit- filled believer. But when one is so filled, the Spirit produces all nine facets of that fruit at the same time. It is His fruit, and being God, He can produce all facets of the fruit in a believer at the same time.

Of course the more that believer grows, the greater his capacity for filling. But a babe in Christ can be filled with the Spirit. It is just that his capacity for filling is small.

There are many more character traits that the Spirit produces in a believer. I want to call them the "fruits" of the Spirit. These fruits are always present, to some extent, in the Spirit-filled believer.

PRAISES TO GOD

Listen to the praises at Pentecost! To be sure, there were people there that were grumbling and accusing the twelve of being drunk. They were the unbelievers. In Acts 2:4, 46-47, the believers were full of joy and praises for God… In Acts 3:8-9, the healed man was walking, and leaping and praising God. He was praising God so loudly, that he got ALL the people's attention. When Paul and Silas were in prison at Philippi in the stocks, after being beaten, they were singing and praising God.

According to Eph. 5:19, there will be the praise of joyful singing. Don't you just love to hear someone sing with joy, making melody in his heart to the Lord. One of the things that I have noticed in my years of pastoring and preaching, is that, when you go to a church where the Spirit has freedom, the singing is lusty, loud, and loving. I love it.

There will be the praise of thanksgiving. Eph. 5:20. Spirit-filled Christians are grateful and thankful Christians. You won't hear a Spirit-filled believer grumbling and complaining. Why? First, grumbling and complaining is sin. (1 Cor. 10:10). If a believer is grumbling and complaining he is sinning and is no longer filled with the Spirit.

A greater reason that the Spirit-filled believer is always thankful in praise is that he believes that God is in control of his life. He has given the Spirit of God freedom in his life to do as He wills. It is the Spirit of God that is working in him, "both to will and to do of his good pleasure" (Phil. 2:13). Note that God is doing His GOOD will, and His GOOD pleasure for your life. How can a believer help but to give thanks and praises for that?

Also there will be humility and harmony and love in the home. (Eph. 5:21-25). This will cause any man to praise God. The husband and wife are submissive to each other. v. 21. The Spirit-filled believer is submissive to all other believers. His wife is a believer. The wife is submissive to her husband in the fear of God. The husband loves his wife like Christ loved the Church. All of the above will bring joy to any home giving cause to praise God. There is also

POWER FOR PRODUCTIVE LIVES

In Acts 1:8, Jesus told His disciples that they would receive power after that the Holy Spirit had come upon them. They would have power to witness to the very ones that they had previously feared and hidden from in the upper room. After they were filled with the Holy Spirit, they went out and preached Jesus boldly, and thousands were saved. They were so productive in their ministry that they were accused of turning Jerusalem upside down. What a blessed accusation. Paul and his followers had so much success that they were accused of turning the world upside down.

It was the norm for the early church to be filled with the Spirit. Today it is almost considered abnormal. But 12 disciples, filled with the

Spirit of God, led a movement that swept through the world, converting sinners to Christ and changing lives. The power of God was upon them. He just filled them with His Spirit.

The primary purpose of power is for service. (Luke 24:46-48). They were to tarry in Jerusalem until that power had come upon them and then, and then only, were they to go forth preaching in all nations. That was a tremendous task but they had tremendous power and they were successful.

The power of God on them in the person of the Holy Spirit gave them a boldness in witnessing, and patience in suffering. Act. 4. They had the Spirit of Wisdom. They had a right spirit. They blessed when they were cursed and persecuted. They turned the other cheek. They went preaching knowing that they would be stoned, beaten, ridiculed, and imprisoned. But none of these things stopped them. Their goal was to be obedient to their calling and commission. They were obedient and they were filled with the Spirit and walked in the Spirit.

They had power to cast out demons when it became necessary. (Luke 10:1, 17-20;

Acts 13, and 16). There are a lot of people today who need deliverance from demons. So many of us have relegated such action to the deceived and deluded.

They had power to make Jesus so real to others, that those others knew that they had been with Him. This is one of the most fruitful things about a Spirit-filled person. He makes Jesus real to others. He makes Jesus real to others because Jesus is so real to him, having been made so by the Spirit of God. Then too there is

POWER FOR PERSONAL RIGHTEOUSNESS

One of the major purposes and ministries of the Holy Spirit is the sanctification of the believer. "[13] But we are bound to give thanks always to God for you, brethren beloved of the Lord, because God hath from the beginning chosen you to salvation through sanctification of the Spirit and belief of the truth: (2Thess 2:13)

The Spirit works in the believer to lead him to be conformed to the image of Jesus Christ. To do this, He comes to dwell in the believer at the time of the new birth. He seals the believer in Christ, and never leaves him nor forsakes him. When the believer is not yielded to the

Spirit, or filled with Him, sanctification is much slower. But when the believer is yielded and obedient, the process goes much faster, and the Spirit-filled believer grows at a tremendous rate. Understanding of the kingdom of God really opens up to him.

According to Eph.5:9,the Spirit bears fruit in the life of a believer more when that believer is living in "goodness, righteousness, and truth." In such a context the believer is being obedient, good, and believing the truth of God's Word. He walks in that truth. Such a walk by "his children" brought joy to the apostle John.

In Gal. 5:22-23, the fruit that the Spirit bears in the believer's life is love, joy, peace, longsuffering, goodness, gentleness, faith, meekness, and self-control. This is the character of Jesus Christ being produced in the life of a believer by the Spirit of Christ. It is righteous living. The longer and the more consistently the believer walks in the Spirit, the more he becomes like Jesus. Oh precious brother, how vital it is for us all to be filled with and walk in the Spirit that we might be a sweet savor of Christ unto God.

There is the work of the Spirit. (Gal. 5:22-24). There is the walk of the Spirit in v. 25, and there is the will of the Spirit in v. 26. Jesus is the example. And there is

POWER FOR PROPER STEWARDSHIP

One of the first things that a Spirit-filled believer recognizes is that God owns all things. (Psa. 24:1-2). Everything on and in this earth belongs to God. It does not belong to the individual who may hold title to it. It belongs to God. He created it for Himself. (Col. 1:16)

I have "owned" several properties in my life. But I was made aware that they were not really mine. God, in His goodness, had just allowed me to be a steward for Him of those properties. You see God owned them before I got there, or any other person that ever held title to them. Now since I have left or sold them, God has allowed someone else to be steward of those same properties. This process will continue. My responsibility is to be a good steward for God of His properties.

God says that the cattle on a thousand hills are His. (Psa. 50:10). Incidentally the thousand hills are His too. This scripture presents us with the truth that God owns everything upon the earth as well as the earth. That includes all of my possessions. I also am a steward of those possessions. I am charged with responsibility of using them for Him to the greatest advantage. The more faithful and wise I am in the use of them the more He entrusts to my stewardship.

A Spirit-filled believer makes his possessions available to God. In Acts 2:44-45, these new Spirit-filled believers did not count anything that they owned was their own. They made it all available to God for Him to use to help those believers who had nothing because of their conversion. They shared all things common.

In Acts 4:32-37, a similar situation occurred. These believers counted none of the things which they owned as their own, but had all things common also. They sold their possessions and brought the proceeds and made them available to all. The apostles made distribution as each person had need. This procedure became so common that the apostles were using all their time making distribution to the needy. There was no time left for the Word of God and prayer. It occasioned the election of the first deacons to do the distribution. Not very many of us make our possessions available to God.

A Spirit-filled person honors God with His tithe. A tithe is one tenth. Biblically it is the first tenth of all of a person's increase. The tithe was to be taken out first, before the costs of living.

The giving of the tithe back to God's work was practiced long before the law of Moses. Abraham gave the tithe to Melchizedek, the high priest of the Most High God. (Gen. 14:20). He gave him tithes of ALL. When the law was given to the people of God through Moses, the principle of tithing was included. It expressed the will of God for His people concerning their stewardship of what He had entrusted them with.

The principle was carried over into the New Testament by Jesus. In Matthew 23:23, Jesus informed the Pharisees that they had their priorities backward. The Pharisees were putting their major emphasis on being sure to tithe everything while they omitted greater matters of love, judgment and mercy. Jesus was not rebuking them for tithing, but for ignoring love, judgment, and mercy. They were still to bring their tithes to God's house.

In Leviticus 27:30 we are told that ALL of the tithe is the Lord's. It is holy unto the Lord. A careful reading of the Bible will reveal that God did not allow man to use His "holy things" for their own use or misuse them without severe consequences.

In Leviticus 27:30 ff, if a person wanted to keep a part of his tithe for any reason, such as a tithe of the herd, he had to give the value of the tithe animal plus one fifth added to it.

In Mal. 3:8-12, we are instructed by God to bring ALL of His tithe into the storehouse of the Lord. To fail to do so was to be robbing God. ALL the tithe is the Lord's. When we don't bring it all, we are keeping for ourselves what is God's. God wants us to prove His faithfulness to us. He says if we bring all of His tithe to the storehouse of the Lord, He will open the windows of heaven, and pour out such a blessing on us we won't be able to use it all. If we obey, He makes things happen in our favor to prosper us to the extent that others will call us blessed.

In 1 Cor. 16:2, God tells us that on the first day of the week, Sunday, the day we go to church, that each of us is to "lay by him in store" in proportion as God has prospered him. Then if each of us brought the tithe of how much God had prospered us, we would all bring an equal amount in God's sight.

You say, "But I can't afford that." The truth is that you cannot afford not to. Not to tithe is to cut off the blessings God wants to give you. Tithing is a matter of testing as to whether or not we really trust God. It is also a test as to whether He can trust us with a lot of this world's goods. Remember that without faith it is impossible for us to please God. (Heb. 11:6). Then it wouldn't matter how good we tried to live, if we didn't have faith in God, we couldn't please Him. But the Spirit-filled man or woman is given the power to tithe and practice good stewardship of all they have by the Spirit of God. It is one of the fruits of the Spirit.

In this chapter we have seen some of the fruits of the Spirit in the life of a believer. In John 15:1-8, we are encouraged by Jesus to be a fruit bearer. It is in the bearing **of fruit, more fruit, and much fruit**, that our heavenly Father is glorified. When you are filled with the Spirit, He is bearing His fruit in your life.

Since you are a believer, why not be filled with the Holy Spirit?

Happy fruit bearing!!!

Chapter 10

The Work of the Holy Spirit Among Sinner and Saint

The blessed Holy Spirit of God is the One Who affects all the facets of our salvation. We are all, saint and sinner alike, dependent upon Him for anything and all things that we know about God and His Word. The Holy Spirit moved men to write the Word. The Holy Spirit reveals the Word to us. His ministry to us is vital.

The Holy Spirit now does all God does in the world. He is God's Agent working the will of the Father in everything. He does a lot more in the world than we will give time and space to here. I want to major on what the Holy Spirit, The Spirit of Christ, God's Spirit, does to bring us to Christ and conform us to His image. In the following paragraphs and pages, I want to share some of what I have learned about the Holy Spirit's work on our behalf.

THE SPIRIT CONVICTS

The Holy Spirit convicts the sinner of his sin, of his need of righteousness, and of the judgment to come. (John 16:8). Except for the Holy Spirit's work in a sinner's life, he would never have a sense of his sin, or his need of Christ, nor could he ever come to Christ. "There is none that seek after God." (Rom. 3:11).

There are many ways that the Holy Spirit does His work in the life of an unbeliever to make him a believer. I will not try to elaborate them all. The Holy Spirit works in the sinner's life to make him aware of his condition. The Spirit may do it through the sinner observing a believer's life that is so different from his. The Spirit may just make him miserable and uncomfortable in his present situation. He may begin by giving him a great hunger for righteousness and a desire to know God. The sinner may observe the heavens and think of God and want to know Him.

The Holy Spirit is not limited in the various ways that He can draw a sinner to Jesus. But He is the One who draws him. When the sinner really begins to hunger for God, the Spirit begins to make Jesus known to him. He may pick up a Bible and read, or he may read an article about Christ. Again, someone may witness to him, or he may decide to go to church.

In a church, the Bible, the witness, or the article, the sinner hears about Jesus as the Savior of mankind. The Holy Spirit reveals Jesus more and more until the sinner is convinced that He is the Christ, the Son of the living God. He is convinced that his sin will send him to hell if he does not turn to Christ. He repents and invites Jesus into his heart. In that moment the Spirit's last work is done in the sinner. Then the new birth occurs.

THE SPIRIT GIVES SPIRITUAL BIRTH

The Spirit births the sinner into the kingdom of God here on earth, and justifies him in heaven in the courts of God. (John 3:3-7; Rom. 3:26). The moment the sinner is born again, he is no longer a sinner, but becomes a saint in the act of the new birth. The new birth takes place on earth in the heart and life of the sinner and immediately the Spirit takes up abode in the new believer's heart.

THE SPIRIT JUSTIFIES

Simultaneous with the action of the new birth on earth, the sinner is justified in heaven. This means that he is declared not guilty of his sin because Christ has borne it for him. He is declared righteous with the righteousness of Jesus Christ because of his faith in Him. (Rom.4 and 5). He is now a child of God and the Spirit's work begins from within.

The Spirit Seals Us In Christ

When the Holy Spirit gives birth to the sinner to make him a child of God and takes up His abode in the life of the new child of God, the Spirit seals the sinner into Jesus Christ. (Eph 1:13). He will never be out of Christ. The promise of scripture is that the Spirit of God will never leave him. (Heb. 13:5). Also the indwelling Spirit is God's guarantee to the new child of God that his redemption will be complete. (Eph. 1:14). Also, in Phil. 1:6, the Word tells us that we have this confidence in Him, that He which has begun a good work in us will also complete it until the day of Jesus Christ. My, what a promise!!

The Spirit Teaches The New Believer

The Spirit now begins teaching the new child of God and will for the rest of his days on earth. He opens the scriptures to him. He reminds him of what Jesus has said to him from the Word of God. As the Spirit takes the babe in Christ and begins His work in him, he begins to grow in the grace and knowledge of our Lord Jesus. Now the Spirit convicts the new believer of any sin or disobedience to Christ. But the new believer has learned that by confessing his sin, he is cleansed by the same blood of Christ that cleansed him to begin with.

The Spirit Guides

Now the new believer is being guided and led by the Spirit of God. (John 16:13). The Spirit begins to show the believer things to come. (v. 14). The Father and the Son begin to really make themselves known to the believer who is living in obedience to the Word of God. (John 14:21, 23). He is now being led by the Spirit of God. (Rom. 8:14; Prov. 3:5-6; Psa. 37:23). What a blessed privilege. How different than when he was a sinner!!

The Spirit Reveals The Deep Things Of God

As the new believer continues to grow in grace and knowledge, the Spirit now is ready to reveal to him the deep things of God. (1 Cor. 2:9-13). As the gospel is read or preached in the power of the Spirit, He begins to open the heart, mind and spirit of the hungry believer. He teaches and reveals the deeper things of God. The new believer begins to compare spiritual things with spiritual, (scripture with scripture) and in so doing discerns the truth and the will of God. Oh, what a blessed thing the Spirit does in this operation!

THE SPIRIT QUICKENS THE WORD IN US

It has been my experience that I can read the same scriptures many times and just get "the ordinary sense" from them. Then one day I read the same scripture and WHAM!! It radiates. It blinks at me like a neon sign. It is now full of new meaning. It becomes personal to me.

In 1961 God led me and my family to New York State to begin new churches. I left a church in South Carolina that was growing. We had just completed our third building program. Everything was new. But God said go to New York. I was sure of it. I went to New York to no church, no salary, no job, and no house to live in. Maybe you think I was crazy. Maybe I was, for Christ.

One day after I had been there several weeks, I was especially down, to the point of weeping. What had I gotten myself into? What was I to do? On that particular day I was beginning a study in Joshua. I read the first nine verses of chapter one through tears. It suddenly came alive to me! It burned in my spirit! It was drawing my attention like a neon sign! It spoke to me as plainly as if God was verbally talking to me!

God was giving us the land! Every place that my foot trod upon was mine! No man would be able to stand before me! I was to be strong and of good courage! I was to observe all of His Word! He had commanded me to be there! He would give me good success! Glory to Almighty God!!! I came out of my chair. I was laughing and crying too. But the crying was for joy and excitement.

What an encouragement that was to me. God kept His Word to me for the next 22 years! I was in a strange land. I had nothing to work with, nothing to invite people to except Jesus. But I went to work with an entirely new attitude and expectancy. We rented an old one-room school building. In 18 months God had filled it with people! We needed more space. God gave us 5.5 acres of land in the city!! In 23 months from arrival we broke ground for a new building. We did not have one dollar. The excavating work was begun with a gift of $20.00 from one of the members. The work never slowed nor stopped until we had the first two units of a five-unit building. God had done it, and in some of the most unusual ways.

We dedicated this lovely church plant and began a mission. From there, God established 28 churches in our area!! I had learned so much! My faith had a shot in the arm that I have lived by for over 40 years! The Spirit of God made the Word of God alive to me to encourage me and make known His will for me.

THE SPIRIT SANCTIFIES US

In 2 Thess. 2:13, God tells us that He has "from the beginning chosen us unto salvation through sanctification of the Spirit, and the belief of the truth."

Now, sanctification has two functions or purposes. First, sanctify means to set apart for God's use. We are now His. The Spirit has set us apart for God's use, for His service. We are no longer our own. He has purchased us by the blood of Jesus Christ and we belong to Him.

The second function of sanctification is to make holy. He convicts us when we sin. He guides us into the way. He teaches us right from wrong. He sanctifies us with His Word, for His Word is truth. He is at work conforming us to the image of His Son Jesus! It may seem slow to you sometimes. You may even grow weary in well doing! But let me tell you. God is never slow according to His calendar. He is always on time. Not ahead, or not behind. He is at work in us accomplishing His good pleasure in us. (Phil. 2:13). Take hope. Praise Him in and for everything! He inhabits the praises of His people!!

THE SPIRIT GLORIFIES JESUS AND MAKES HIM REAL

In John 16:14, the Word says, "He shall glorify me: for He shall receive of mine and shall show it unto you." Jesus is speaking of the Spirit in the context.

The Spirit is always presenting Jesus in the true light. He does this by simply telling the truth about Jesus. When Jesus is so presented, He is glorified. He is perfect in all His motives. He is perfect in all His works. He is perfect in His obedience to the Father. He is perfect in His love for the Father and for the world. He is perfect in living His life. He is perfect in His sacrifice. Hallelujah!! What a Savior!!

Not only does the Spirit glorify Jesus, but He presents Him in such a way that He becomes real to the Spirit-filled believer. He becomes as real as your wife or neighbor. This is only true to the Spirit-filled believer. He can do this because the only motive of the Spirit-filled believer is to know Jesus better, and to believe and obey Him. He does become real.

THE SPIRIT EMPOWERS US

Of course that is the main thrust of this book. The Spirit indwells us from the day of our new birth. He is always resident in our life. BUT WE HAVE TO MAKE HIM PRESIDENT. We do this by the processes explained in this book.

THE SPIRIT COMFORTS US

In John 14-16, Jesus refers to the Holy Spirit, Whom He would send when He went away, as the Comforter and Counselor. The Spirit knows all about us. He knows our "down sitting and our uprising." He knows all of our hurts. He knows when we are down and discouraged, as I was when I first went to New York. And in all these situations, the Spirit comforts and consoles us.

He reassures us of God's love and care. He reminds us of our place and position in Christ. He teaches us about our inheritance in Christ and what is involved. When things get worse or heavier than we seem to be able to bear, He makes a way of escape that we may be able to bear it. He reminds us that Jesus is coming to take us out of this mess and home with Him. Then He tells us to comfort one another with these words. How much more powerful and happier the church would be if we all comforted one another rather than criticized one another.

THE SPIRIT PRODUCES THE CHARACTER OF CHRIST IN US

The goal of the believer is to be conformed to the image of Jesus Christ, the only Son of God. In the Spirit-filled believer the Spirit produces the fruit of the Spirit in the believer's life. This fruit of the Spirit is the character of Christ.

There are nine facets of the fruit of the Spirit; love, joy, peace, longsuffering, goodness, gentleness, faith, meekness, and self control. These are character traits that every concerned child of God desires and seeks after. But we cannot attain unto this character on our own. It is not the work of man. It is the work of the Spirit in the believer producing the character of Christ.

Too often many believers strain and struggle in an effort to produce one of these character traits. We work so hard at it. We set our wills. We stubbornly and steadfastly go at the work of achieving several facets of the Spirit's fruit. Regardless of how valiant we are in our efforts--- and real often when we think we are about to achieve--- we have a big fall. All of our efforts have been in vain. But the omnipotent Spirit of God easily and naturally produces all facets of His fruit simultaneously when we are totally surrendered to Him.

THE SPIRIT LIBERATES US

"Where the Spirit of the Lord is, there is liberty." (2 Cor. 3:17). The Spirit of God liberates us from the law of Moses. Speaking of the law of Moses, the Bible says that "the law is holy, the commandment is holy, and just and good...... For we know that the law is spiritual..." (Rom. 7:12, 14).

Paul tells Timothy that "the law is good, if a man use it lawfully." (1 Tim. 1: 8).

He then explains that the law is not for the righteous man, (counted righteous by faith in Christ) but for the ungodly and sinner. Paul says in Rom. 3:19 that it is by "the law that we have a knowledge of our sin."

So the law is our schoolmaster to lead us to Christ by showing us that we are sinners and need a Savior. After the law has brought us to Christ we are free from the law. In Gal. 5:1, we are told to "Stand fast therefore in the liberty wherewith Christ has made us free."

The Spirit has liberated us from the law of sin and death and condemnation.

"For the law of the Spirit of life in Christ Jesus has made me free from the law of sin and death. For what the law could not do in that it was weak through the flesh, God sending His own Son in the likeness of sinful flesh, and for sin, condemned sin in the flesh: that the righteousness of the law might be fulfilled in us who walk not after the flesh, but after the Spirit," (Rom. 8:2-4). "For brethren, we have been called unto liberty; only use not liberty for an occasion to the flesh, but by love, serve one another." (Gal. 5:13)

THE SPIRIT OF GOD RAISES US FROM THE DEAD.

All men from Adam to the present have died, with the exception of Enoch and Elijah. It is appointed unto man once to die. But those of us who have our faith and trust in Jesus and His shed blood have a blessed hope. That hope is in the Lord Jesus' personal return to earth to rapture the entire church. Death is the last enemy to be totally conquered. It is not the enemy of our soul and spirit, but of our bodies which must die if Jesus tarries.

But about the resurrection, the Bible says, "But if the Spirit of him that raised up Jesus from the dead dwelleth in you, he that raised up Jesus from the dead shall also quicken your mortal bodies by his Spirit that dwelleth in you." (Rom. 8:11).

This will all happen when our Lord Himself descends from heaven with a shout, the voice of the archangel and the trump of God. When Jesus calls forth the dead, the Spirit of God will change their old dead bodies into bodies fashioned like His glorious body. Our bodies will rise up to meet the Lord in the air. We will then be reunited, the new body with our soul and spirit which God will bring with Him. 1 Thess. chapters 3 and 4, and Phil. 3:21.

The Spirit of the living God has such a vital role in the life of the believer from the beginning to the resurrection. This being so, should not each of us seek to build an intimate relationship with the Spirit? By being filled? But instead many believers commit sin against the Holy Spirit.

Since you are a believer, why not be filled with the Holy Spirit? Happy Working!!!!

Chapter 11

Sins Against the Holy Spirit.

All of the sins that man commits are against Almighty God, Creator of our universe. But scriptures present some sins as being against the Holy Spirit. We all know that the Godhead consists of God the Father, God the Son, and God the Spirit. The three names for the same Person are used interchangeably. Yet, they have different functions and offices, so to speak. But it is still one God, and it is the same God working in either of the three names.

In this chapter we want to focus on sins against the Holy Spirit as the third person of the Godhead, and the One Who is working among us now. We know that there is a sense in which all sin is against the Holy Spirit, for He is God. We don't really understand the Trinity. But the Bible seems to point out that some sins were sinned against the Holy Spirit.

RESISTING THE HOLY SPIRIT

Men of both the Old and New Testaments are accused of resisting the Holy Spirit. Stephen, one of the first elected deacons, filled with the Spirit, was speaking to his contemporaries about Jesus being the Christ. They refused to hear his message which was being inspired by the Holy Spirit. Stephen then made this statement. "Ye stiff- necked and uncircumcised in heart and ears, ye do always resist the Holy Ghost: As your fathers did, so do ye." (Acts 7:51)

It is my conviction that all people who resist the message of the Word of God are resisting the Holy Spirit. The Spirit is at work in every believer seeking to conform him or her into the image of Christ. Too many of us have a stubborn streak in us. We want to do our thing when we want to do it. In so doing some of us are "receiving the grace of God in vain."

When we resist the work of the Holy Spirit in our life, it could be that we will never be what we could have been if we had yielded to Him. This is sad. I am not sure that the Holy Spirit will ever give us that chance again. Then again, He may.

It is a dangerous thing to resist the work of the Holy Spirit in our life. It has consequences in two ways. We may not ever become what God's perfect will is for us. Then we may have to suffer consequences as the Spirit works in our life to make us willing. Another sin against the Holy Spirit is like spiting Him.

TO DO DESPITE TO THE SPIRIT OF GRACE.

The scriptures tell us that, "He that despised Moses' law died without mercy under two or three witnesses: Of how much sorer punishment, suppose ye, shall he be thought worthy, who hath trodden underfoot the Son of God, and hath counted the blood of the covenant, wherewith he was sanctified, an unholy thing, and hath done despite unto the Spirit of grace?" (Heb. 10:28-29) Webster gives the meaning of "despite" as showing contempt for or defiance of someone or something.

It appears that the scripture is talking about a believer here. I say this for several reasons: 1. They counted the blood of the covenant by which they were sanctified an unholy thing. Unbelievers have not been sanctified by the blood of Jesus. 2. He insulted the Holy Spirit. 3. The Lord will judge His people. This seems to indicate that the one sinning so was a child of God.

I don't profess to know all there is about this. I know that a believer can cross God's deadline of grace and God will take him on home. Only God knows what sin He takes a believer home for. At our very best, we are simply speculating. But I do know that we who have been cleansed by the blood of Jesus Christ must hold His blood sacrifice as a very holy and sacred thing. To do otherwise is to slap God in the face with our disregard for the greatest of sacrifices ever made.

GRIEVING THE HOLY SPIRIT

A third sin against the Holy Spirit is to grieve Him. In Ephesians 4:30 we read, "And grieve not the Holy Spirit of God, whereby ye are sealed unto the day of redemption."

The text goes on to say that we are to put away bitterness, wrath, anger, clamor, evil speaking and malice from among us. These sins grieve the Holy Spirit who is living within us and whose attitude is the very opposite. I believe when we hold un-forgiveness, resentment, hatred, jealousy, covetousness, and lust, we are seriously grieving the Holy Spirit.

The Holy Spirit is God. He has the right to determine what the character of a believer is to be. He has described this in His Word. When we disobey it hurts our Comforter and Counselor. Entirely too few of us give this a thought or a second thought. We just act according to our will and our desires, both of which are fallen. Only when we are walking in the Spirit and living in the Spirit are we pleasing to God.

QUENCHING THE SPIRIT

A fourth sin against the Holy Spirit is to quench Him. "Quench not the Spirit." (1 Thess.5:19). To grieve the Spirit and quench the Spirit are similar. I believe they have a very distinct difference. Grieving the Spirit seems to be sins of commission. They are the negative things that we do in disobeying God. They are doing the things that He tells us not to do.

Quenching the Spirit, on the other hand, seems to be not doing what we should be doing. It is disobeying what God is inspiring and motivating us to do. It is failing to give witness to a certain person at a certain time. It may be the failure to help a person who is down and in need. It is refusing to exercise the faith that the Holy Spirit is seeking to build in us by tithing or any other Biblical expression of faith in God. It is pouring water on the fire that God is building under us!!

TEMPTING THE SPIRIT

Still another sin against the Spirit is to tempt Him, such as in lying to Him. In Acts 5:1-10 we have an account of this sin and its consequences. It seems that Ananias and his wife Sapphira had sold a piece of property. It seems that they wanted some of the praise and adoration that had been going to Barnabas and others who had sold property and given the money to the disciples for benevolent purposes.

Their sin was that they wanted to keep part of the sale price for themselves, but make the church believe that they had given all of the purchase price. So they brought a part of the proceeds and gave them to the apostles. Peter, being filled with the Spirit and having the spiritual gift of knowledge, perceived immediately what had happened. So Peter said, "Ananias, why hath Satan filled thine heart to lie to the Holy Ghost, and to keep back part of the price of the land?....You have not lied unto men, but unto God." A few hours later Sapphira came in, having agreed with Ananias to try to deceive the apostles by pretending to have given more than they did. Peter said to her, "How is it that ye have agreed together to tempt the Spirit of the Lord?" (Acts 5:3,4,9).

Ananias' and Sapphira's sin probably included several wrongs. First off, they assumed that either the Holy Spirit wouldn't know what they were doing or He would be so proud of them that it didn't matter. Secondly, they were guilty of exaggeration any way you look at it. They had planned to give part and make others believe that they had given all. It seems that they were more interested in impressing men than God.

Thirdly, they were seeking the praise of man more than the praise of God. No doubt they had heard the praises of the people toward Barnabas when he had sold a farm and given it all to the apostles. They wanted some of that praise without earning it.

Fourthly, in their pretense they lied to the Holy Spirit. Seeking to keep the truth from God's people comes close to lying to God. The effort is useless anyway. God knows all about us, all that we think, do, say, or intend to do. Why do God's people think that they can deceive those in the work of God and escape the consequences?

Ananias and Sapphira paid an awesome price. They both lost their lives immediately. They did not die because they gave only part of the sale price to the apostles. They died because their intent was to deceive God's leaders. In doing so they tempted the Holy Spirit and lost their lives. God tells us to speak every man truth with his neighbor. He tells us to lie not. He is unhappy with us when we lie.

Vexing The Spirit

Isaiah accused the people of his day of vexing the Spirit. In Isaiah 63:10 we read,

"But they rebelled and vexed his Holy Spirit: therefore he was turned to be their enemy, and he fought against them."

Israel, God's chosen and beloved had forgotten the goodness and the kindness of their God to them. They forgot how He had redeemed them and brought them safely through the wilderness. So they rebelled against God in order to do their own thing. They may have been saying something like, "It doesn't matter how we worship, just so we do." Every man may have been doing what was right in his own eyes. The point is that they vexed God's Spirit and made God angry. Needless to say, they, too, paid the consequences. God became their enemy!! What a poor choice of enemies!!

Denying The Holy Spirit Control

Another sin against the Holy Spirit is to deny Him control of our life. God commands us to be filled with the Spirit. To ignore that or refuse to be filled is rank sin and rebellion. Jesus sent His Spirit from the Father to indwell us, lead us, guide us, teach us and so on.

To not yield ourselves to His control to the best of our knowledge and ability is sin. We are the losers every time.

In the same family of sin against the Holy Spirit is the matter of contempt for the work of the Spirit. I have known so-called believers who have looked with contempt on the actions and behavior of other believers. Some of such actions may have been wrong, but I seriously doubt that the loud praising of God with joyous actions is wrong. We are commanded to do so many times in scripture.

Blaspheming The Spirit

The last and most serious sin against the Holy Spirit that I will include here is to blaspheme Him. In Matt. 12:31-32 we read of the sin which only sinners can commit,

"Wherefore I say unto you, All manner of sin and blasphemy shall be forgiven unto men: but the blasphemy against the Holy Ghost shall not be forgiven unto men."

"And whosoever speaketh a word against the Son of man, it shall be forgiven him: but whosoever speaketh against the Holy Ghost, it shall not be forgiven him, neither in this world, neither in the world to come."

At first glance it seems that blaspheming the Holy Spirit is attributing the work of the Spirit to the devil. And it certainly seems to include that. The only hindering thing here is that it is very easy for a believer to attribute the work of the Spirit to the devil. This would mean that he or she could never be saved. That runs contrary to too many scriptures, such as John 10:28; Rom. 5:1-10; Rom. 8:1-4; Col. 1:13-14, and Phil. 1:6 and others.

I do not believe that a believer can from his heart commit this sin for which there is never forgiveness, in this world or the next. It is an easy sin to commit. Every sinner on his way to becoming a believer runs the risk of committing this terrible sin. If I read Matt. 12:23-28 correctly, it was what they were thinking as much as what they were saying to which Jesus responded. Jesus was performing miracles that people might believe that He was the Son of God. It was the work of the Holy Spirit by Whom He was performing the miracle of casting out demons. This was to reveal Jesus as the Son of God and Savior.

The text says that Jesus, knowing their thoughts, answered them. The common people were saying as a result of seeing the miracles that Jesus did that He was the Son of David. This was a common term used for the Messiah. The Pharisees could not allow that to get by or it would destroy their plan, purpose, and position. It "must be" refuted. So they accused Him of working by the power of Satan.

I believe that there is a parallel to this in Heb. 6:1-6.

" Therefore leaving the principles of the doctrine of Christ, let us go on unto perfection; not laying again the foundation of repentance from dead works, and of faith toward God. Of the doctrine of baptisms, and of laying on of hands, and of resurrection of the dead, and of eternal judgment. And this will we do, if God permit.. For it is impossible for those who were once enlightened, and have tasted the heavenly gift, and were made partakers of the Holy Ghost, and have tasted the good word of God, and the powers of the world to come, if they shall fall away, to renew them again unto repentance; seeing they crucify to themselves the Son of God afresh, and put him to an open shame."

I believe that these verses also relate to the unpardonable sin of refusing to believe or acknowledge Jesus as the Son of God the Savior of the world. The writer of Hebrews names five things that the people falling away were exposed to. They were enlightened, tasted the heavenly gift,(not received it), made partakers of the Holy Ghost, (not received Him, or birthed by Him, or been sealed by Him), and have tasted the good word of God, and the powers of the world to come.

The above is exactly what an unbeliever experiences on his way to becoming a believer. The Holy Spirit is at work in him to reveal Jesus as the all sufficient Savior. The Holy Spirit leads the unbeliever right up to the "top step" of "tasting the powers of the world to come. I believe that at this point the unbeliever can "see" all he needs to see to accept Christ as his Savior. If after experiencing all this he says no and turns away, the Bible says it is IMPOSSIBLE to renew him again unto repentance. In order to do so the Son of God would have to be crucified again. That would put Him to an open shame. And that is not going to happen. He died ONCE and for all, and made one sacrifice for sins forever.

If the above text applied to a believer, the one falling away could never be saved again. It would be impossible. Once saved and then lost, no more salvation for that one!! The thought also negates so much of God's purpose, plan, and promises of salvation. A person would live continually in morbid fear of committing this sin. I believe that ultimately, the blasphemy of the Holy Spirit and Heb. 6:1-6 sin are one and the same.

Sinning against the Holy Spirit is an awful thing. It brings so much chastening, sorrow, and pain. Whereas being filled with the Spirit and walking in the Spirit bring all that a believer could possibly want to make his life full and meaningful. It is a wonderful thing to live your life for a revealed purpose of God. Such is the portion for the Spirit-filled person as he walks with God. So then,

Since you are a believer, why not be filled with the Holy Spirit? Happy filling!!!!

Chapter 12

The Inspiration of the Holy Spirit

The Holy Spirit inspiring the children of God is a vital part of the Kingdom of God and His work here on earth. I did not include it in the WORK OF THE HOLY SPIRIT chapter because I wanted to give it a wider treatment. Apart from His vital ministry among us, the church would be in a state of confusion. The devil would see to that.

The Holy Spirit's work among us is much wider than I have included in this book. Also His work of inspiration cannot be fully treated here. But I would like to try to deal with those parts of His ministry of inspiration that relate to our being filled with, living in, and walking in the Spirit.

THE HOLY SPIRIT INSPIRED THE WORD OF GOD

I include the inspiration of the Word of God here because it is so vital and important to the promises of God and how we respond to them. We can see the power of God and the wisdom of God in His creation. We can see the acts of God in history. But the only place that we find God's relationship with man is in the holy scriptures. It is in the Word of God---and only there--- that we can find His instructions to us. Therefore the Word of God and its inspiration is vital to the Spirit-filled life.

It is important that the child of God know that God's Word is true in its entirety. If he believed that only certain parts are inspired, he could not know what to believe or trust in. His or some other person's mind would become the highest authority. But since the Word of God--- which is the Bible we have--- is all divinely inspired, we know that we can trust and act upon any or all of it. I believe this to be fundamental in a believer's walk being pleasing to God.

In 2 Timothy 3:16 we read, "All scripture is given by inspiration of God, and is profitable for doctrine, for reproof, for correction, and instruction in righteousness: that the man of God may be perfect, thoroughly furnished unto all good works."

In this verse we see that the man of God is thoroughly provided with God's Word to do all of his works.

God breathed into Adam and he became a living soul. Just as certain is the fact that God has breathed His Word into the minds of the prophets or writers. In so doing it became the living Word of God. God most certainly inspired more than thoughts and concepts. I believe that He inspired words. Words express and define concepts. Therefore, if words change, concepts change. It doesn't seem feasible that an all-wise God, knowing man, would have left such an uncertain word for men to have to determine what is the Word of God and what isn't.

We read: " Knowing this first, that no prophecy of the scripture is of any private interpretation. For the prophecy came not in old time by the will of man: but holy men of God spake as they were moved by the Holy Ghost." (2Pet.1:20-21)

Holy men of God spoke as they were moved by the Holy Spirit If only the thoughts and concepts of the Word were given them, then those thoughts and concepts would of necessity have to be interpreted by them in order to write them down in words. But the scriptures say that they were not of private interpretation or origin. These bold men wrote as they were inspired, and moved by the Holy Spirit. In my understanding this does not violate the personality or talents, or knowledge of the writer anymore than a person writing on two different typewriters violates the personalities and capabilities of the typewriters. He simply writes within the capabilities of each typewriter. So I believe that God inspired each prophet or writer within the personality and capabilities of that writer

According to the scriptures, those holy men did not always understand what they were writing:

1 Peter 1:10-12 " Of which salvation the prophets have enquired and searched diligently, who prophesied of the grace that should come unto you: 11 Searching what, or what manner of time the Spirit of Christ which was in them did signify, when it testified beforehand the sufferings of Christ, and the glory that should follow. 12 Unto whom it was revealed, that not unto themselves, but unto us they did

minister the things, which are now reported unto you by them that have preached the gospel unto you with the Holy Ghost sent down from heaven; which things the angels desire to look into."

In the above quoted verses, the prophets did not understand about the grace they were writing about. They inquired and searched about what and to whom they were writing. But the Spirit of Christ which was in them inspired them to write what they wrote even if they did not understand. This seems to indicate that God inspired the words they were to write.

The apostles of the New Testament claim a similar inspiration for themselves. We read in 2 Peter 3:1-2, " This second epistle, beloved, I now write unto you; in both which I stir up your pure minds by way of remembrance: That ye may be mindful of the words which were spoken before by the holy prophets, and of the commandment of us the apostles of the Lord and Saviour:" Peter seems to be saying that he had a commandment from the Lord Jesus to write what he did.

The apostle Paul stated several times in the New Testament that the things he was writing were the commandments of the Lord. Truly ALL scripture is inspired of God and is absolutely trustworthy. You may also want to check on these scriptures: (1 Cor. 14:37; 1 John 4:6; Acts 7:38; Rom. 3:2; 1 Pet. 4:11).

Not only did God inspire the prophets and writers, but he speaks to us.

THE HOLY SPIRIT SPEAKS TO US

According to our Lord Jesus, the Holy Spirit speaks to the church. In Revelation chapters 2 and 3 He says, "He that hath ears, let him hear what the Spirit saith to the churches." It seems that individuals are also meant here for it says, "He that hath an ear".

The Spirit is speaking to the churches, and the churches are made up of individuals. Also in this same text it says, "He that overcometh," another reference to individuals. It seems that the Holy Spirit speaks to the whole church, but only certain individuals heard and responded.

This does not mean that individuals hear an audible voice. God is able to speak to us in many ways. He speaks through His Word. He speaks through circumstances. He speaks through our deep and continued impressions of heart, mind and spirit. But however He speaks, He never speaks contrary to His Word. When people say that they have prayed about it and have peace about it, and then go contrary to His Word, God has not spoken to them giving them His approval. He may allow them to go ahead with the disobedience, but He doesn't approve it. God never contradicts His Word.

I have often heard people say, "God has told me" to do this or that when the thing they proposed to do was diametrically opposed to His Word. We can be sure that God did not tell such and such. He just doesn't instruct us to go contrary to His Word. His Word is settled forever in heaven and does not change. I am always subject to obedience to it.

When we assert that God speaks to us as individuals, it is not to infer in any way that His message to us is on a par with His messages to the prophets and writers of holy writ. We are fallible beings and are often subject to hearing the wrong spirit. Here again, the best way to test if it was God's voice we heard is to check it against His Word. He may speak to us with a word that is not in His Word, but never contradicting His Word.

The Holy Spirit also directs our paths.

THE HOLY SPIRIT DIRECTS OUR PATHS.

" Trust in the LORD with all thine heart; and lean not unto thine own understanding. 6 In all thy ways acknowledge him, and he shall direct thy paths." (Prov. 3:5-6) According to this verse, God promises to direct our journey through life if we trust in Him with all of our heart and do not trust our own wisdom

I wonder if the reason that so many of His children do not enjoy this advantage is that they don't trust Him with all their heart. They rather choose to follow their own understanding. Very often the way of the Lord seems unwise by human and worldly reasoning. In such cases faith and trust must override our reasoning so that we can follow God's way.

[13] Howbeit when he, the Spirit of truth, is come, he will guide you into all truth: for he shall not speak of himself; but whatsoever he shall hear, *that* shall he speak: and he will shew you things to come. John 16:13 Jesus tells that the Spirit will guide us .

" There is a way which seemeth right unto a man, but the end thereof are the ways of death." (Prov. 14:12) This verse tells us that there may be a way that seems wise to us, but that way, if followed, will destroy us.

Isaiah 55:7-9 "7 Let the wicked forsake his way, and the unrighteous man his thoughts: and let him return unto the LORD, and he will have mercy upon him; and to our God, for he will abundantly pardon. 8 For my thoughts are not your thoughts, neither are your ways my ways, saith the LORD. 9 For as the heavens are higher than the earth, so are my ways higher than your ways, and my thoughts than your thoughts."

What can we do when it seems that all we know seems to lead us in a way in opposition to God's Word. It is wise to realize that God doesn't think and operate as we do. We are fallible. He is infallible.

The apostle Paul is a good example of this. In Acts 16:6-7, they were forbidden to preach the Word in Asia. When it seemed right for them to go into Bithynia, the Spirit forbade that also. How the Spirit let them know that they were not to preach the Word in either place we do not know. Neither is it important as to how He forbade them but we know that He did. It seems that the Spirit has a mind and will of His own as to where He wants us to go and when. The fact that God did not want Paul and his party to go to either of these places does not mean that He did not want someone else to go there. The command of God is to go into all the world and preach the gospel. It just wasn't His will for Paul to go at that time.

I was pastoring a church in South Carolina that was growing to the extent that we had had three building programs in five years. God spoke to me in the midst of that to go to New York State to begin a new church with a mother and three daughters. He did this by showing me the need there and burdening my heart to meet that need. He also spoke to my wife, who was back in South Carolina, at the same time He spoke to me in New York. When I returned from this trip to visit our mission work in New York she already knew that we were going.

Paul got directions as to where the Spirit did want him to go after he was forbidden to preach in Asia and Bithynia. God spoke to him in a vision of a man in Macedonia requesting him to come there. Paul immediately knew that God was directing his path to where He had people ready to respond. As it turned out, this was one of Paul's greater works. I am glad that Paul was sensitive to the Spirit's direction and we must be too.

In Acts 8:26-40, Philip is another example of the Spirit's guidance. He was having a powerfully successful evangelistic crusade in Samaria. Multitudes were being saved. Lives were being changed. In the midst of all this, an angel of the Lord appeared to him and instructed him that he was to leave Samaria and go down into the desert toward Gaza. He obeyed and on the way saw an Ethiopian returning from Jerusalem. Then the Spirit spoke to him and directed him to go join himself with the man in the chariot and preach Jesus to him.

Here again in obedience to the Spirit's direction Philip won the man to Jesus and baptized him. It seems that even before the Ethiopian left to go on his journey to Ethiopia the Spirit had caught Philip away. I am not sure I understand the phrase "caught away Philip." I do know that it was His power in action to take Philip where He wanted him to be. The point in all this is that the Spirit speaks to us in directing our paths in a way that we can understand.

Then again the Holy Spirit inspires us in prayer.

THE HOLY SPIRIT INSPIRES US IN PRAYER

" Likewise the Spirit also helpeth our infirmities: for we know not what we should pray for as we ought: but the Spirit itself maketh intercession for us with groanings which cannot be uttered. 27 And he that searcheth the hearts knoweth what is the mind of the Spirit, because he maketh intercession for the saints according to the will of God." (Rom. 8:26-27)

In these verses God seems to be telling us that because of our weakness we don't always know how to pray about a given situation. When this happens the Holy Spirit comes to our rescue. He searches our hearts and leads us in prayer according to God's will.

I suspect that most of you have experienced a like thing with me. A situation arises that I just don't know how to pray. In spite of my own searching for a prompting from God, conviction as to how I ought to pray eludes me. The above text tells me that the Spirit helps me at this point. He intercedes for me. He does this with groanings which cannot be uttered or spoken. To me this eliminates tongues at this point. Tongues can be uttered or spoken even if no man understands them. Paul had a prayer language in tongues. I know that some people pray in tongues according to their testimony. But if tongues is what is meant here, then the Spirit could not intercede for the mass majority of believers because we do not speak in tongues.

The point is that when the Holy Spirit intercedes for us the burden of prayer is lifted. We have peace in our heart that we have cast this burden on Jesus that He might sustain us. To illustrate, on a certain occasion I suddenly had a tremendous burden to pray for the life of one of my sisters. I did not know that she was sick or hospitalized. I did not know how to pray. I just knew that I should. The Spirit interceded for me, and though I did not know what had transpired, I knew that God's will would be done. As it turned out, I found out later that she was at the point of death. The doctors had said that she wouldn't live at the same time the burden came on me. She got well and lived many more years. I thank God so much for the wonderful ministry of the Holy Spirit. What a wonderful help to the child of God!!

Also the Holy Spirit inspires our witness to Jesus Christ.

THE HOLY SPIRIT INSPIRES OUR WITNESS

" They were aware of it, and fled unto Lystra and Derbe, cities of Lycaonia, and unto the region that lieth round about: And there they preached the gospel. And there sat a certain man at Lystra, impotent in his feet, being a cripple from his mother's womb, who never had walked: The same heard Paul speak: who stedfastly beholding him, and perceiving that he had faith to be healed, said with a loud voice, Stand upright on thy feet. And he leaped and walked." (Acts 14:6-10)

" And from thence to Philippi, which is the chief city of that part of Macedonia, and a colony: and we were in that city abiding certain days. 13 And on the sabbath we went out of the city by a river side, where prayer was wont to be made; and we sat down, and spake unto the women which resorted thither. 14 And a certain woman named Lydia, a seller of purple, of the city of Thyatira, which worshipped God, heard us: whose heart the Lord opened, that she attended unto the things which were spoken of Paul." (Acts 16:12-14)

In both of the above texts, it appears that Paul was directed and inspired by the Holy Spirit as to where and to whom to bear witness. In South Carolina, I pastored a rural church. The parsonage had its own septic system which at one time was out of order. I was in the back yard digging a new ditch for a drain line. I kept feeling impressed to go to a certain man and bear witness to the saving grace of Jesus Christ. I made all kinds of excuses. "I was too busy on a critical job. The man was too hard and would not listen. He had only been to church a few times and was not "ready" to be saved".

But God did not let up on His impression on me. It only got stronger. Finally, unable to resist any longer I got out of the ditch, showered and changed clothes. I went to the man's house with a dread of rejection. I shared the gospel with him and his wife. Before I ever finished sharing I knew this was of God by their actions and countenances. Both of them were gloriously saved and became workers in the church. I was so glad that the Spirit had inspired me to go and that I went.

In another situation, I was traveling from Myrtle Beach, S.C. to Greensboro, N.C., when I came upon a hitchhiker. I felt strongly impressed to pick him up, something I didn't usually do. Under the inspiration of the Spirit I shared with him the gospel and the plan of salvation. He related that he had been hungering and searching for God and he too was wonderfully saved. I firmly believe that the Holy Spirit inspires us as to whom we should witness and when.

THE SPIRIT INSPIRES US TO RECONCILIATION

" And all things are of God, who hath reconciled us to himself by Jesus Christ, and hath given to us the ministry of reconciliation; 19 To wit, that God was in Christ, reconciling the world unto himself, not imputing their trespasses unto them; and hath committed unto us the word of reconciliation." (2 Cor. 5:18-19) God reconciled to us to Himself by the death of His Son Jesus Christ. He then imparts to us the ministry or responsibility of being reconciled with others. It is also our responsibility to reconcile others with Him

In many places in the Word of God, we are instructed to forgive and be forgiven. We are told to be reconciled to whomever we are at odds. Far too many believers do not heed the moving of the Holy Spirit in these matters for one reason or another. Their heart is hardened. The longer one puts this off the harder their heart becomes. Then it is tougher to do whatever is needed to be reconciled.

I have never been at odds with another person that the Spirit did not impress me to make reconciliation with that person. And believe me there have been many. It is a very difficult thing for a man and his wife to live together without being crossways with each other at times. Often in my early Christian life I would let these things go too long. I learned that to walk in the Spirit I had to obey the Spirit as He tugged at my conscience to be reconciled with her. I also learned that I should take the initiative in this reconciliation, whether I was right or wrong. To do so works wonders. Any time that I fail to obey the Spirit to be reconciled I am grieving Him. If I am to daily enjoy His fullness and blessings I am to be obedient to His inspiration.

Entirely too many of God's children live as if there was no Holy Spirit. Their life is not much different than the life of the unsaved according to their own testimony. This ought not to be. When Jesus went back to heaven, He sent the Holy Spirit as our Paraclete, our counselor, our Comforter, our Guide, our Teacher, our Strength, and our Leader. Jesus sent Him because He knew that without Him, we could do nothing. Left to our devices we would be in a great mess. He is and His Word is all that we need to walk with God and be pleasing to Him. He is more than enough to make us successful in our life and our ministry. He wants to glorify the Father through His Son, Jesus Christ. In order for Him to do this in our lives, we must be surrendered to Him on a continual basis. This we do by keeping every sin confessed to date. Then by faith we must ask to be filled with the Holy Spirit again.

So then, if you are a believer, why not be filled with the Holy Spirit? Now!!

Happy filling and living!!!

Chapter 13

The Conclusion

So then, what is the conclusion of the matter?

It is a fact that every sincere believer wants to live pleasing to the Lord. This is good and as it should be. It is never easy, but it is possible. We know definitely that one cannot live according to the desires of the old nature and please God. "So then they that are in the flesh cannot please God." (Romans 8:8) The word "flesh" in this scripture means the old nature that we are born with. To keep from living according to the old nature, one needs to walk in the Spirit.

"*This* I say then, Walk in the Spirit, and ye shall not fulfil the lust of the flesh."

(Gal 5:16) In order for one to walk or live in the Spirit, one must first be filled with the Spirit. Being filled with the Spirit is what the main part of this book is about.

God has commanded us to be filled with the Spirit. "And be not drunk with wine, wherein is excess; but be filled with the Spirit; Speaking to yourselves in psalms and hymns and spiritual songs, singing and making melody in your heart to the Lord; Giving thanks always for all things unto God and the Father in the name of our Lord Jesus Christ;" (Eph 5:18-20). To be pleasing to God then, one must be filled with and walk in the Spirit.

We also know that one must live by faith to be pleasing to God. "But without faith *it is* impossible to please *him*: for he that cometh to God must believe that he is, and *that* he is a rewarder of them that diligently seek him." (Heb 11:6) To live by faith is to believe what God has said in His Word and obey it.

One can see from the scriptures quoted above that one cannot live by his old natures and please God. One can also see that living in such a manner as to please God, one must live by faith. In order to live by the new nature and faith, it is necessary to know what to believe. This knowledge comes from God's Word---the Bible.

In order to know how to apply the teachings of the Bible to one's life, one must study the Bible repeatedly. There is a vast difference in reading the Bible and studying the Bible. To study the Bible effectively one needs to study it by subjects. For example, study the Bible by the subject of marriage, divorce, Christ's return, the Spirit-filled life, what happens to believers when they die, obedience, and every other subject which one will encounter in life. When one learns what the Bible teaches about any subject, it can be applied to daily living by obedience through faith. I have spent the last fifty-six years of my life reading and studying the Bible by subject. It has enabled me to live by faith in confidant assurance, that when I obey what the Bible says, I am pleasing to God. You can also.

There really aren't any shortcuts to this process for the results to be profitable. Such study has the added benefit of our learning what the promises of God to us are. It is necessary to know what God has promised in order to claim those promises by faith. God prospers His children who trust and obey Him in all things.

In partnership with the study of God's Word is the matter of obedience and faith. One may be better off not to know what God's Word says and then disobey it. A major part of the Bible is given to informing us of God's commands and laws with the admonishment to obey them. Obedience to God's Word is absolutely necessary to live the Spirit-filled life. This means obeying ALL of the Word. Far too many of us treat God's Word like we do a food line in the cafeteria. We go through the line looking at all the food and then choosing what appeals to us. Such is not an option with the Bible. Partial obedience is in fact disobedience..

Let us look at a well known example of disobedience in 1 Samuel 15. God had instructed King Saul of Israel to destroy the Amalekites and all that they had. " Now go and smite Amalek, and utterly destroy all that they have, and spare them not; but slay both man and woman, infant and suckling, ox and sheep, camel and ass." (1 Sam 15:2-3)

But Saul only partially obeyed. " But Saul and the people spared Agag, and the best of the sheep, and of the oxen, and of the fatlings, and the lambs, and all *that was* good, and would not utterly destroy them:" (1 Sam 15:9) When confronted by Samuel for not carrying out God's command, Saul began to tell Samuel he had saved the best to sacrifice to God.

"And Saul said unto Samuel, Yea, I have obeyed the voice of the LORD, and have gone the way which the LORD sent me, and have brought Agag the king of Amalek, and have utterly destroyed the Amalekites. But the people took of the spoil, sheep and oxen, the chief of the things which should have been utterly destroyed, to sacrifice unto the LORD thy God in Gilgal. And Samuel said, Hath the LORD *as great* delight in burnt offerings and sacrifices, as in obeying the voice of the LORD? Behold, to obey *is* better than sacrifice, *and* to hearken than the fat of rams. For rebellion *is as* the sin of witchcraft, and stubbornness *is as* iniquity and idolatry. Because thou hast rejected the word of the LORD, he hath also rejected thee from *being* king" (1 Sam 15:20-23)

A casual reading of the 15th chapter of 1 Samuel will reveal God's displeasure at Saul's disobedience and its consequences. We see that in order to live pleasing to God it is necessary to be obedient to His Word.

Obedience to the things we have learned in our study of God's Word is easier when we associate with others who are doing the same thing. They become an encouragement and not a hindrance to learning and obedience. When we spend much of our time with those who have no interest in the things of God, they are a hindrance and a drag to our learning and obedience. Most people have a tendency to behave like those they associate with. I have found if I associate with believers who are living the Spirit-filled life I am continually reminded of my need to do the same. This does not mean that we are to withdraw from society. It does mean that I need to spend a lot of times with others of like faith and experience for strengthening.

Another important action that helps to live pleasing to our Lord is sharing with others what God is doing in our lives. I am not sure all that happens in us when we share, but I do know that sharing with others what God is doing in my life helps confirm it to me. This has been true about my salvation experience, my being filled with the Spirit, and many others things in which God was dealing with me.

Yet another exercise that helps in living pleasing to our Lord is the matter of offering the sacrifice of praise and thanksgiving to God. " By him therefore let us offer the sacrifice of praise to God continually, that is, the fruit of *our* lips giving thanks to his name." Heb 13:15

It is Jesus that we are to speak our praises through. We also need to remember that God inhabits the praises of His people. When we are busy singing God's praises for His goodness to us we don't have the time to complain.

The Spirit-filled believer is always giving thanks to God for everything. "And be not drunk with wine, wherein is excess; but be filled with the Spirit; [19] Speaking to yourselves in psalms and hymns and spiritual songs, singing and making melody in your heart to the Lord; [20] Giving thanks always for all things unto God and the Father in the name of our Lord Jesus Christ;" (Eph 5:18-20)

The Spirit-filled believer can even gives thanks to God for the unpleasant things in life. He does so because he knows God is working the bad with the other things in life for our good. "And we know that all things work together for good to them that love God, to them who are the called according to *his* purpose." (Romans 8:28)

Yes, it takes faith to give thanks for the bad in one's life. The Spirit-filled believer is living by faith. He believes just what God said in the above verse. Because God loves the believer and purposes to conform him to the image of Jesus, He uses good and bad to build character in us. May I illustrate? I like pie. But I don't like some of the ingredients that go into a pie. I do not like raw eggs, shortening, and some the other ingredients. I do not like the heat that it requires to cook the pie. But I love pie because it is good. Our lives are like that. When the master Pie Maker mixes all the experiences, both good and bad, of our lives together and adds the right amount of heat we turn out to be something He likes.

God is also pleased when we do good deeds for and give to others. "But to do good and to communicate forget not: for with such sacrifices God is well pleased." (Heb 13:16)

When the King James version of the Bible was written the word "communicate" meant to give or share. God is saying in Heb. 13:16 that He is well pleased with our good treatment toward others. This is especially true of our help with the needy.

Finally, it pleases our Lord for His children to watch for His return. Paul tells Titus to look for Jesus' coming." For the grace of God that bringeth salvation hath appeared to all men, teaching us that, denying ungodliness and worldly lusts, we should live soberly, righteously, and godly, in this present world; Looking for that blessed hope, and the glorious appearing of the great God and our Saviour Jesus Christ;" (Titus 2:11-13)

The importance of our looking for His return is revealed in the frequency of its mention in scripture. Scholars count 1,845 references to His coming in the Old Testament. It is mentioned 318 times in the New Testament, once for every 25 verses.

Jesus told us repeatedly to watch for His coming. He gave us many signs that indicate that His coming may be near. It is easy to see why He wants us to expect His return at any time. It has a sanctifying affect on us. " Beloved, now are we the sons of God, and it doth not yet appear what we shall be: but we know that, when he shall appear, we shall be like him; for we shall see him as he is. ³ And every man that hath this hope in him purifieth himself, even as he is pure." (1 John 3:2-3)

The above verse also tells us that on that occasion, we shall see Him as He is. What a joy that will be to every child of God that has walked in the Spirit. That person will not be ashamed when his Lord returns. "And now, little children, abide in him; that, when he shall appear, we may have confidence, and not be ashamed before him at his coming." (1 John 2:28)

It has been 19 centuries since many of these promises were made and He hasn't returned yet. Shouldn't we just give up watching for Him. Peter tells us the the delay is because our Lord wants all men to come to repentance and faith. " The Lord is not slack concerning his promise, as some men count slackness; but is longsuffering to us-ward, not willing that any should perish, but that all should come to repentance." (2 Peter 3:9)

So we must wait with patience for His coming. But He is coming so that we can be with Him where He is. Our salvation is much nearer than when we first believed. " Be patient therefore, brethren, unto the coming of the Lord. Behold, the husbandman waiteth for the precious fruit of the earth, and hath long patience for it, until he receive the early and latter rain. Be ye also patient; stablish your hearts: for the coming of the Lord draweth nigh." (James 5:7-8) "And that, knowing the time, that now *it is* high time to awake out of sleep: for now *is* our salvation nearer than when we believed." (Romans 13:11)

The Spirit-filled person finds joy in living all of these things. It is joy because he knows that he is pleasing to God in so doing.

Since God has told us exactly how to be filled with the Spirit, and since God has commanded us to be filled, and since the greatest joy in life for the believer is to be filled with and walk in the Spirit, why not experience what pleases God and enjoy it?

Happy filling!!

Some Recommended Books On The Spirit-Filled Life

1.	The Key To Triumphant Living	Jack Taylor
2.	After The Spirit Comes	Jack Taylor
3.	Victory Over The Devil	Jack Taylor
4.	The Simplicity Of The Spirit-filled Life	L.L.Letgers
5.	They Speak With Other Tongues	John and Elizabeth Sherrill
6.	The Saving Life Of Christ	Major Ian Thomas
7.	The Release Of The Spirit	Watchman Nee
8.	The Normal Christian Life	Watchman Nee
9.	The Spiritual Man (3 Vol.)	Watchman Nee
10.	Living Dangerously	Stuart Briscoe
11.	The Fullness Of Christ	Stuart Briscoe
12.	Rivers Of Living Water	Ruth Paxson
13.	Life On The Highest Plane	Ruth Paxson
14.	The Shantung Revival	C. L. Culpepper
15.	The Holy Spirit, Who He Is, And What He Does	R.A.Torrey
16.	The Holy Spirit and Missions	J. B. Lawrence
17.	Practicing The presence Of Christ	Brother Lawrence
18.	The Spirit Of Christ	Andrew Murray
19.	The Spirit Controlled Temperament	Tim LaHaye
20.	Absolute Surrender	Andrew Murray
21.	Let's Quit Fighting About The Holy Spirit	Peter Gilquist
22.	Born Crucified	L. E. Maxwell
23.	Revolution Now	Bill Bright
24.	The Christ Life For Your Life	F. B. Meyer
25.	The Bible (The Best)	Holy Spirit
26.	Dealing With The Devil	C. S. Lovett